THE
SAINTS
THE
SUPERDOME
AND THE
SCANDAL

THE SAINTS
THE SUPERDOME
AND THE SCANDAL

Dave Dixon

Foreword by Peter Finney

PELICAN PUBLISHING COMPANY

GRETNA 2008

The word "Pelican" and the depiction of a pelican are trademarks
of Pelican Publishing Company, Inc., and are registered in the
U.S. Patent and Trademark Office.

Library of Congress Cataloging-in-Publication Data

Dixon, Dave, 1923-
  The Saints, the Superdome, and the scandal / Dave Dixon ; fore-
word by Peter Finney.
      p. cm.
  ISBN 978-1-58980-493-7 (hardcover : alk. paper) 1. New Orleans
Saints (Football team)—History. 2. Superdome (New Orleans, La.)—
History. 3. Dixon, Dave, 1923- I. Title.
  GV956.N366D59 2008
  796.332'640976335—dc22

                                    2007048297

Printed in the United States of America

Published by Pelican Publishing Company, Inc.
1000 Burmaster Street, Gretna, Louisiana 70053

Contents

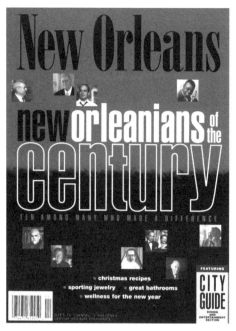

New Orleans Magazine cover, "New Orleanians of the Century," December 1999. (Photo courtesy *New Orleans Magazine*)

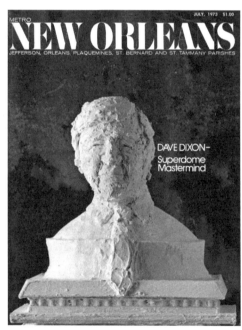

New Orleans Magazine cover, "Dave Dixon—Superdome Mastermind," July 1973. (Photo courtesy *New Orleans Magazine*)

Foreword

When the next history of New Orleans is written, there has to be a chapter devoted to Dave Dixon. Without such a chapter, no history of the Big Easy would be complete. You can come up with all kinds of lists, dealing with movers and shakers; with music and food; with political leaders, good and bad; with saints and sinners; with people who made a difference, large and small, spanning generations, shaping a skyline. You do all that and Dave Dixon has to be in the mix, way up there.

"At my age," an eighty-three-year-old Dave was telling me, "I weep easily." He's saying this as the Saints, an NFL franchise he brought to his city, were preparing to play their first home game of the 2006 season in the Louisiana Superdome, that giant mushroom of a building Dave dreamed into reality. This would be no ordinary football game. It would be an extraordinary moment full of symbols: New Orleans rising from the dead, in prime time on your TV set, at the very spot in the days following Katrina where a nation had watched horrible scenes of a city swimming, of its people begging for help.

"You bet I cried," Dixon recalled about watching the horror on television. "The Superdome had become a symbol of our nightmare. But as awful as those scenes were—and they made me weep—I know that the Superdome saved lives just by affording shelter to desperate people who were chased from their drowning homes." Such sentiments were typical Dave Dixon, always in search of sunshine in the face of, in this case, an unprecedented disaster.

"Think about it," he said. "A year later, the Superdome became a post-Katrina miracle, like a nightmare being washed away, sort of like our Eiffel Tower coming back to life. What a moment! Good people whose lives were changed forever were sitting there telling one another, 'Are you ready for some football?' Our Superdome was out there, front and center, leading a city's comeback."

Because of the hand and vision of Dave Dixon, a comeback of sorts for our great old city began on All Saints' Day 1966 when city officials gathered at the Pontchartrain Hotel to hear Commissioner Pete Rozelle announce that New Orleans would be part of the NFL. Dave not only had used his salesmanship skills in selling the city to the powers of pro football, he had used them in selling Tulane officials on Tulane Stadium becoming the interim home of the Saints while he and Gov. John McKeithen were selling Louisiana voters on a domed stadium. Dave was sitting in the rear of the Patio Room that day when Rozelle came up to him and said, "Thank you, Dave, for making all this possible." Whereupon, Dave, already looking ahead to an upcoming statewide vote on a domed stadium, said: "Thank you, Pete, for helping us sell a new stadium." The Superdome would open in 1975 and, in time, host Super Bowls, Final Fours, and a visit by the Pope, not to mention countless mega-entertainment events, conventions, and trade shows, enough to generate billions of dollars for the city.

In John McKeithen, Dave met the governor of his dreams, a rabid LSU football fan who told Dave, "In this state, telling voters football is king is akin to a political wisdom." Dave likes to tell the story of the day he made his domed stadium pitch to a governor who was lying back in his chair, eyes closed, feet propped up on a table. "I talked for thirty minutes about what a great thing it would be for the city, the state. I was trying to sell a man from north Louisiana where plenty of voters looked down on our town. I'm talking away and it looks like the governor is fast asleep. Finally, I stop. The governor opens his eyes. He says, 'Is that it?' I nod. The governor gets up, raises his fist, slams his hand on the table, and shouts: 'By God, we're gonna build that sucker.'"

It was built for a final tab of $163 million, a project with some delays, some infighting, but without a hint of scandal. Dave would carry a cardboard model of his dream around the state. In forty-six days, he would make seventy-six speeches to groups, large and small. The final vote was five to one in favor of building that has become an architectural wonder frozen into the city's skyline. It makes you wonder if anyone had a greater impact on the city than the man who never stopped dreaming.

Dave is the man who founded the United States Football League, a temporary burr under the saddle of the National Football League and one that would produce countless stars in the NFL. He's the man who cofounded World Championship Tennis with Lamar Hunt, bringing colorful outfits to what had been a white-dress-only sport for men and women. He's the man who continues to dream, at the moment about a "fan ownership football league" that could not miss, in Dave's words, of "succeeding overwhelmingly." "I'm absolutely convinced," says Dave, "that sports teams have become so civic in nature they should be majority-owned by hometown fans everywhere. And not by individual owners."

A crazy idea? Crazy idea? That's what so many out there were saying back in the days New Orleans was on the outside, its nose pressed to the window, looking in on the big time. Crazy idea? That's what they were saying when people were laughing at the thought of the little Big Easy building a much bigger, much better dome than the Astrodome.

What follows is Dave Dixon's story. It's the story of a senior citizen who has found his way to the fountain of youth. Someone who weeps easily. And dreams endlessly.

—Peter Finney,
National Award-Winning Sports Columnist,
New Orleans Times-Picayune

Acknowledgments

My book is a story about New Orleanians and Louisianians . . . and people everywhere. A ghost writer almost certainly would write more eloquently than I, but I feared that some of the passion that my wife, Mary, and I feel for the people of our city and our state inevitably would be lost. So, I decided that every single word, thought, and experience herein would originate with this passionate New Orleanian and Louisianian.

This book would not have been written without the assistance and constant encouragement of my distinguished nephew, Julian L. McPhillips, Jr., a prominent Montgomery, Alabama, attorney. I do not have a better friend, anywhere.

CHAPTER I

September 25, 2006

There they were, our post-Katrina New Orleans Saints, perennial NFL losers, but beloved by their fans. It was Monday Night Football, and ESPN's all-time record television audience was poised to watch the Saints do battle against the Atlanta Falcons in our spectacular, back-from-the-dead Louisiana Superdome. Never has there been such a football moment anywhere!

Amazingly, our Saints were an impressive 2 and 0 after road victories over the Cleveland Browns and the Green Bay Packers. The Falcons also were 2 and 0, including a big road win over the 2006 Super Bowl preseason favorite Carolina Panthers. A perfect setting!

Wonder of wonders, our Saints took control immediately, winning handily! The more secure our win, the more we beat-up Saints fans worked ourselves into an ever wilder frenzy. Never have I seen a happier, more joyous crowd than that magnificent Monday night!

I remember thinking that a story for the ages was being played out before our eyes. A true epic. By the time that Monday night game ended, I had elevated it in my mind to one of the great moments of history. "My God," I said to myself, "We Katrina-exhausted New Orleanians are living testimony to the indomitability of the human spirit!"

My beautiful Mary Dixon, a native of Memphis, whose ardor for everything New Orleans knows no bounds, said to me when I decided to make "September 25" this book's opening chapter: "Sweetheart, your readers are football fans, not historians. Tell them what you told me when that game was over."

Overcome by the moment, I had told my wife, "Tonight,

sweetheart, September 25, 2006, our New Orleans Saints became a New England-type franchise, solid contenders from now on with Sean Payton as the head coach and Mickey Loomis as the general manager. At long last our Saints showed the world that they will be a good football team for years to come." If that isn't an epic moment for New Orleanians, what is?

But let's go way back in time and see how I, a New Orleans native, stumbled into creating our New Orleans Saints and then our Louisiana Superdome, a perfect combination of New Orleans and Louisiana.

CHAPTER II

The Birth of a
Great Sports Fan

For whatever reason it fell my lot in life to organize the civic effort to bring New Orleans into major league sports through our New Orleans Saints and to visualize and bring into being our magnificent Superdome. It might be said that everything began at Touro Infirmary on Prytania Street in New Orleans, my birthplace, on June 4, 1923.

For the first twelve years of my life, I lived at 7925 Plum Street, one and a half blocks from Carrollton Avenue, a major New Orleans Uptown thoroughfare, two blocks from the old Poplar Theatre on Willow Street where I saw cowboy movies every Friday night for ten cents, and two blocks from the public library at Willow and Carrollton, where I devoured *Boy's Life* magazine, *The Saturday Evening Post,* and Robert Louis Stevenson, Mark Twain, and Jack London books. I attended Robert E. Lee School, one block farther. It was just a ten-minute (seven-cent) streetcar ride to Heinemann Park and our Southern Association baseball club, the beloved New Orleans Pelicans. The Pels won numerous pennants under a genius of a manager named Larry Gilbert.

In those days I knew and climbed virtually every backyard fence in the neighborhood. Those backyard fences were so familiar because most residents of that area had fig trees, and in many cases I was their contracted climber and picker. They got half the figs I picked; I sold the other half in the neighborhood and at Mr. Kelly's grocery on Oak Street. I averaged about six dollars per week, a princely sum for a young boy during the early to mid-1930s. I bought hundreds and hundreds of Big League Chewing Gum cards with all that fig money. I wish I had those cards today!

At Lee School, I remember well Miss Agnes Pollet, my seventh-grade teacher and aunt to the great World Series pitcher for the St. Louis Cardinals during the 1940s, Howard Pollet, a neighborhood friend. Miss Pollet was young and beautiful, and all my friends were in love with her, as was I. But my favorite teacher was Miss Bertonniere (Hilda, I believe), also very pretty, my sixth-grade teacher who taught English and played tennis with me at the Audubon Park courts on several occasions. Miss Bertonniere, the sister of Mayor Robert Maestri's wife, convinced me that I could become the school's valedictorian "if only you would stop cutting up and laughing so much."

I decided to follow Miss Bertonniere's advice, mainly because I had a tremendous crush on classmate Dorothy Ecuyer. I thought correctly that top grades would impress this young beauty, four months older than I and destined incidentally to become a Tulane homecoming queen. Sure enough, I became boy's valedictorian at Lee School, and Dorothy Ecuyer was named girl's valedictorian. As Dottie put it years later, "David Dixon was the first and only boy I allowed to carry my books home from school." What a Romeo! In later years, whenever she visits New Orleans from her home in Florida, I kid Dottie that she was too old (by mere months) for me. I also joke that in the seventh grade she scored higher grades than I only in hygiene and deportment.

What a chump I was to carry Dorothy's books for her to her home on Sycamore Street, in the opposite direction from Lee School than our home on Plum Street. But maybe that's what happens to an eleven year old experiencing his first great love in life. Dottie Ecuyer Moore, a champion in school and in life, is my friend to this moment. I had good taste even then.

Babe Ruth

One of my earliest memorable experiences in life and in sports occurred during the Chicago World's Fair in the summer of 1933. I had just turned ten when our parents decided to take my sister, Eleanor, and me to the Chicago Fair, a great, wonderful, exciting family experience.

David Frank Dixon, Dixon's father, 1938.

Stuart Dixon Clay, Dixon's mother, 1960.

Seventy-four years later there are three things that still stand out in my mind about that visit, almost as if they occurred yesterday. Sally Rand, the world-famous fan dancer (also known by some as a semi-striptease artist), was performing at the fair. When I had told my punk little friends at home that I was going to the World's Fair, they all said, "Man, you gotta see Sally Rand! She does a fan dance that my dad said will blow you out of your mind!" At age ten I had no idea why someone would be blown out of his mind by a person dancing with a bunch of fans, but I was intrigued nonetheless.

Actually, I had never heard a single thing about Sally Rand from my parents, so I had a feeling that her dance was something "bad." Standing outside Sally Rand's theatre my mother said immediately that Sally Rand's fan dance was "not for little boys and girls," which piqued my interest even more. I really wanted to see what was behind those fans. No dice. We never saw Miss Sally Rand perform. Of course, I couldn't let on to that fact when I returned home, so I told my friends that it was "nothing much." I added, "She's overrated." How could I tell them that I never got even a glimpse of the famous Sally Rand?

The second thing I remember so vividly occurred when we went swimming in Lake Michigan on a warm, sunny afternoon, and I hit the water for the first time. I knew immediately that I had never felt anything quite that cold in my life, solidifying my belief that Yankees not only talked funny but were "strange," except, of course, the New York Yankees. I knew, too, that I never wanted to leave New Orleans, where the water was nice and warm. I was going to live in New Orleans all my life. I am still here, a New Orleanian to my toenails!

My third memory about that Chicago World's Fair will stay with me as long as I live. The New York Yankees, Babe Ruth's team, came to town for a three-game series with the strongly contending Chicago White Sox at famous old Comiskey Park, including a spectacular Sunday doubleheader. This was the first "crucial series" in Chicago since the infamous 1920 World Series when the White Sox and "Shoeless Joe" Jackson apparently threw the series to their National League opponent. This thrown World Series was the biggest sports story in Chicago history and is still bouncing around a bit, even today.

In 1933, the White Sox were in first place for the first time since the days of Shoeless Joe, and the ballpark was rocking. It was the first sellout in thirteen years at the great old landmark, and my father had tickets for the two of us, father and son, no mother, no sister. "Just men," he said. All of Chicago was waiting for the New York Yankees and the biggest star in the history of sports, even by today's standards, the great "Babe" Ruth. We had excellent seats, a box near the Yankees' dugout. I had such total faith in my father that I never asked how we got such prime tickets.

The first game of the doubleheader was about twenty minutes away when an usher came up to me and said, "Come with me, son." I looked to my father, who said, "Son, you're going to see Babe Ruth. If you can get his autograph on your baseball, ask him to sign it with his full name, just to be different." The next thing I knew I was standing about ten feet in front of the Yankees' dugout, a skinny, tall, ten-year-old kid with almost solid freckles and huge ears. I absolutely froze as I recognized (from my collection of Big League Chewing Gum cards, I had them all) Babe Ruth, Lou Gehrig, Bill Dickey, Earle Combs, Red Ruffing, Lefty Gomez, Frankie Crosetti, Tony Lazzeri, and their great manager, Joe McCarthy.

Paralyzed with awe and wonderment, I couldn't move. Suddenly, I heard a booming voice, "Hey, sonny boy, come on down here and see the old Babe." It was Babe Ruth, the Bambino, the Sultan of Swat, the idol of America, particularly of every little kid in the country, especially this little kid. I stumbled over bats, even stepped on the shoes of Lou Gehrig. When I apologized, Mr. Gehrig laughed, saying, "Don't worry about it, son. I have big feet."

When I finally reached The Babe, he picked me up, put me in his lap, and asked me where I was from. I managed to ask him to sign my official American League baseball with his full name, which he did: George Herman "Babe" Ruth, going almost completely around the ball. I ended up with almost all of the Yankees signing that ball.

That much-prized ball survived in good shape until I joined the Marine Corps in early January 1942 a few weeks after Pearl

Harbor. By the time I got home in 1945, my ball had disappeared. I had a hunch that my little step-brother, Louis H. Clay, Jr., had something to do with it, but my mother asked me to promise not to speak to him about it. There had been many a time as a young boy when I tried to retrieve a baseball lost in one of the big "sewers" seen on just about every street in New Orleans. Sometimes I was successful, sometimes I wasn't, but I figured my kid step-brother had "borrowed" my ball for pitch and catch, and it went down one of those sewers, never to be seen again. Years later a friend at Sotheby's in New York told me that a George Herman "Babe" Ruth baseball might be worth millions. But probably not mine. Those signatures were fading, even before World War II.

The Yankees won both games of that doubleheader, knocking the White Sox out of first place. The highlight of that momentous day (the Yankees won a close first game) came late in the second game. The Yankees were killing the White Sox, something like thirteen to one, when Ruth came to bat during the eighth or ninth inning. Hall of Famer Jimmy Dykes, the White Sox player-manager third baseman, was signaling frantically to Ruth, indicating he wanted him to bunt, daring him to bunt, eventually catching Ruth's eye. The Babe just laughed. Immediately Dykes turned his back and walked several steps into left field, shouting to his shortstop to do likewise; he obliged. Now the game was on, and what was left of the huge crowd realized that a fascinating bit of by-play was taking place between Ruth and Jimmy Dykes. Today, Dykes would be fined heavily.

On the first pitch, Ruth held out his bat as though he were going to bunt, then swung mightily, hitting a huge foul ball deep into the right field stands' upper deck. The crowd oohed and aahed.

Dykes persisted, again stepping back into left field. This time The Babe hit an absolutely perfect bunt down the third-base line. I can see him now, his back to us, taking those mincing little steps of his as he beat it out to what was wild, wild cheering, hilarity, and laughter. Ruth took a standing ovation, taking off his cap at first base, waving his cap at the crowd. The cheers lasted for a full two minutes, Ruth taking several bows, taking his cap off with each bow. Babe Ruth took bows better than anyone in history.

Thirteen years later, sometime in 1943, I was a young navigator-bombardier second lieutenant in the Marine Corps, reading the *Los Angeles Times* one morning when I spotted a column on Babe Ruth written by Braven Dyre, sports editor of the *Times*. About halfway through the column, these lines, or something like them, appeared: "Ruth was a wonderful, highly intelligent athlete. For example, he never threw to the wrong base in his entire career from his position in right field, often throwing out base runners who could not believe his cannon of an arm. And he never bunted, not once in his whole career."

Mr. Dyre must have meant *sacrifice* bunt. I was able to locate him via long distance from San Diego, even during wartime, and I told him my story of a ten-year-old kid from New Orleans who watched Ruth beat out a bunt at Comiskey Park. Braven Dyre was a very nice man, and he wrote a nice little correction a day or two later, using my name. Made me something of a minor celebrity in my outfit.

A Crushing Blow

My father, David Frank Dixon, known as Frank Dixon, was also a great sports fan, particularly fond of football. He and I might spend a football weekend of Fortier High versus Jesuit on Friday night, Tulane (then a national power) on Saturday afternoon, sometimes LSU in Baton Rouge that night via a "football-special" train, and the Loyola Wolfpack (pretty good, coached at one time by the great Clark Shaughnessy) on Sunday afternoon. Needless to say, I grew up as a huge football fan, probably the equal of the north Louisianian John J. McKeithen, who became governor in 1964 by defeating our family friend Chep Morrison in a very close election.

From all reports, my father was a brilliant business leader, the founder in 1927 and president-chairman of the Great Southern Box Company, a major employer for those Depression days.

Dixon as a student at Georgia Military Academy, 1938.

Great Southern prospered even during the Depression, so my parents bought a beautiful home in 1935 at the corner of Palmer Avenue and Marquette Place.

I attended Fortier High School for two years, then transferred to Newman when my parents could afford private school. By 1938 my father felt that World War II was coming and military training would be helpful, so I was enrolled for my senior year at Georgia Military Academy (GMA), now known as Woodward Academy, considered by many as Atlanta's best prep school today, as it was pre-World War II.

Little did I know that a crushing blow awaited me. That summer, 1938, my dear, handsome, athletic, six-foot-two father, who seemed to his son to know everything about everything, my great friend, my football companion, my total hero, and a heavy smoker was diagnosed with advanced lung and colon cancer at age forty-five. He died within days at Touro Infirmary, where I had entered the world fifteen years earlier. My family was devastated. After all these years, he is still on my mind every day of my life.

Yet, off to GMA I went, a very dreary soul. I enjoyed GMA and their championship football team and made pretty good grades, actually winning a state essay contest, which pleased my English teacher, Capt. Francis Hulme. I did particularly well in trigonometry and college algebra, everything except chemistry, where my grades were okay but not great, as my mother and sister readily pointed out.

Because I was the youngest boy in our graduating class by almost a full year, Colonel Brewster, the headmaster, a little tough and strict but a good person, recommended that I return to GMA for another year of college preparatory work. He explained that I had the grades and test scores for Annapolis or West Point or for a top eastern college, almost any one I chose, but at age fifteen I needed a little more age and maturity. When he asked me what I wanted, I said, "Colonel, I like it here at GMA, and I like Atlanta, but I want to go home to New Orleans, where I intend to live the rest of my life. And I'm going to go to Tulane." When asked why, I answered, "Colonel, I am embarrassed to admit this, but I want Tulane because their football team is loaded for the 1939 season!" (Besides, I was so unsophisticated that I had no comprehension of the superiority of schools like Harvard, Yale, and Princeton). Sure enough, Tulane went undefeated that year, losing a mythical national championship to unbeaten Texas A&M in the dying moments, 14 to 13, in 1940 in the Sugar Bowl on a highly disputed, apparently illegal scoring play.

I was hooked on New Orleans and football forever, following the example set by my father, an Ole Miss alumnus. When I asked him once why he rooted for Tulane even against Ole Miss, he said, "Son, that's easy. I went to school for four years at Oxford, but I intend to live a lifetime in New Orleans."

My mother remarried in late 1939. Her new husband, Louis H. Clay, was a Ford Motor Company executive headquartered in New Orleans with Louisiana, Mississippi, and parts of Alabama as his geographic area of responsibility. A widower, Louis Clay was a good man who had a nine-year-old son of his own, Louis H. Clay, Jr. I was pleased for my mother, who had been devastated and made terribly insecure by my father's early death.

For whatever reason, aroused patriotism, restlessness, or insecurity at losing a wonderful father so cruelly and unexpectedly and perhaps in a sense losing the full attention of a loving, good mother—for all of those emotions—I enlisted in the Marine Corps as a buck private in late December 1941, shortly after Pearl Harbor and as I was completing the first semester of my junior year at Tulane. Through a lot of good luck, after boot camp at San Diego, I was assigned to the First Marine Aviation Wing at North Island Naval Air Station in Coronado and into Gen. Roy Geiger's headquarters. This brought me into direct, daily contact with this greatest of World War II Marine Corps generals and his executive officer, Col. Louis Woods.

General Geiger and Colonel Woods took me under their wing, becoming father figures to me, and eventually sent me off to St. Mary's Pre Flight with a record book of all 5s (tops), which helped steer me through Navigator-Bombardier School at Hollywood, Florida, from which I emerged as a Marine Corps second lieutenant.

Dixon in his Marine uniform, 1941.

A minor knee injury from landing maneuvers at Del Mar, California, was aggravated by another such injury while I was awaiting orders and assignment. All of this led to surgery, limited duty at Kingsville, Texas, Naval Air Station and an eventual discharge shortly before the end of World War II. So I survived the war, but so many of my great Marine Corps buddies lost their lives that it changed my life forever in many ways, perhaps leading me toward a strong interest in public affairs to which I had never paid much prior attention.

A Tulane Fish Story

My wife, Mary Dixon, insisted that I tell the story of a little-known, hilarious academic misadventure during my freshman year at Tulane back in 1939, even if personally embarrassing. I have kept this little bit of nonsense secret for years, disclosing it only to a very few close friends. Mary insisted I share this story so that people would be "aware of the wild, crazy imagination that ultimately produced the New Orleans Saints and a Louisiana Superdome and the wild, crazy good luck that turned an F into an A and a crummy old railroad yard into Buster Curtis's masterpiece of a Superdome."

Anyone who attended Tulane's College of Commerce and Business Administration during that era will remember the famous Dr. Harvey Lee Marcoux, who taught freshman English and business English so well and so effectively that he had become a legend even to this very young freshman. I must admit that I was dismayed on my first day in his class, a Friday in mid–September, as he handed out a list of ten widely varying topics about which we must write one-thousand-word themes, one due each week. The first paper was due the following Monday.

Didn't Dr. Marcoux know that the preseason #3-ranked Tulane football team was to play #2-ranked Fordham University (a prewar national power from New York City, made famous by Vince Lombardi's "Seven Blocks of Granite") that very Saturday? How the hell could I write a one-thousand-word theme on Sunday? I'd still be exhausted from bringing the mighty Green Wave home victoriously (we won, big time) on Saturday afternoon, plus celebrating on Saturday night. Besides, the Tulane golf team always played together on Sundays. Obviously, I had important social conflicts that weekend.

But it wasn't too tough. The ten topics included seven or eight titles with which I was reasonably familiar. I was able to scratch out one thousand words over that first weekend, for which I received a hard-earned B. Friends told me that a B was very good because the legendary Dr. Marcoux "almost never" handed out As, maybe two or three per year.

There was one title among the ten about which I knew absolutely nothing: classical music. Naturally, I put off classical music until last, the due date finally arriving in late November. Well, my social life was so strenuous (after being away from New Orleans at a military boarding school) that I still had not found time to visit the library to research my final topic . . . and the paper was due the next morning.

I had one ace in the hole, a freshman fraternity brother, Allen "Zeke" Martin, who was an absolute whiz on classical music with an extensive collection of phonograph records of great symphony orchestras. So, at about 10 P.M., with the paper due at 9 A.M. the next day, I engaged my friend in conversation (the usual things such as coeds and football), carefully leading up to classical music. Finally I said, "Zeke, everybody in the fraternity admires your knowledge of classical music. What would you say is your favorite classical composition?" (rather professionally phrased, I thought). Zeke answered immediately, "Beethoven's Fifth Symphony." The only problem was that I thought he had said, "Fish Symphony"!

I was taken aback, but I didn't want to betray my total ignorance to a fellow freshman, so I said, "Beethoven was Austrian, was he not?" Zeke replied, "No, he was German, but he spent much of his professional life and early summers in Vienna." So, I went home and sat before my typewriter pondering how could I possibly write one thousand words about such a topic. Finally, I started writing, and the words just poured out. In desperation I invented "an Austrian uncle, Otto Von Beethoven, a learned, aristocratic, cultured old gentleman" with whom young Ludwig spent joyous boyhood summers in the music capital of the European world.

"It was there," I wrote, "that young Beethoven rested in the wondrous, softly relaxing Vienna Woods, sometimes dozing off as breezes filtered through the magnificent, towering oaks, cedars, and pines. The fishes played gleefully, jumping from brooklet to brooklet, ever leading to the mighty, mystical Blue Danube, as they joined the mainstream currents of Europe's great river." All of this, I stated confidently, was creating the dramatic, powerful strains of his monumental, even immortal, Beethoven's Fish Symphony. On and on, and on and on. One word after another, one line after another.

At 9:00 A.M. I turned in the theme based on Beethoven's Fish Symphony, then walked over to the bookstore on campus, where my buddies would be having "a Coke under the Oak" and exchanging B.S. Within a few minutes someone said something that told me that I had made a dreadful, unpardonable mistake. It wasn't "Fish," it was "Fifth." I was ill! How could I have been so monumentally stupid?

Immediately I rushed back to grand old Gibson Hall, determined somehow to retrieve that paper. I approached Dr. Marcoux's graduate assistant, a very nice gal named Elvia Hamilton, and said with a desperately mustered straight face, "Elvia, I made a number of typos [the whole stupid paper] on the classical music assignment because my typewriter is on the blink, so the paper I turned in this morning is all screwed up. My sister is not using her typewriter, a good one, and she just told me that I may use it. May I retrieve my paper? I'll have it back within the hour."

Elvia said, "David, I'm so sorry, I've already turned in all the papers to Dr. Marcoux. Don't worry, he'll understand your problem. He likes you." She was nice and very kind, but nice couldn't rescue this now desperate young freshman.

Dr. Marcoux was a fabulous teacher, a prodigious worker, all business. He even had a personal conference every two weeks or so with each of his students to review their papers. I lived in dread of my upcoming conference a few days away.

My conference finally arrived. As I entered his little office, he began laughing. A healthy laugh. He then said, "Mr. Dixon, I had no idea that you had such a vivid imagination. Your Fish Symphony paper is the cleverest piece of satirical writing I've seen in a while." With that he took out a red crayon and wrote a big A at the top of my thousand-word theme. I was speechless, still fearing the worst, not quite believing what was happening. Was he kidding me?

Frankly, it took me at least ten years to tell this ridiculous story to anyone, but finally I told it one day to my seat mate on an airliner. A Metropolitan Opera soprano, for goodness sakes! She laughed uproariously off and on for ten or fifteen minutes.

I learned my lesson. I have put in my library research time faithfully ever since, even on topics about which I am already well informed, using both Tulane and Loyola libraries extensively and the main public library downtown. My only excuse so many years ago was that I was barely sixteen years old, and, admittedly, my vast knowledge of fine music in 1939 was confined to such classics as "Chatanooga Choo Choo."

Golf and Mary Dixon

I began to play golf with my father's encouragement at about age ten. On my twelfth birthday I shot a 75 at the old Audubon Golf Club while playing with my dad, the first time I beat him. I would later hold the competitive course record, 62, for many years. Having emerged as City Prep School Champion at age thirteen at Fortier High School, by age eighteen I might have been close to being a pretty good player. However, World War II and more than three years with little or no play, plus becoming mostly a weekend player after the war, eliminated whatever slim chance I might have had of becoming a tour-quality player or even a top amateur.

I know now that my golf game would never have been good enough to play professionally, but it did lead me toward Miss Mary Coyle Shea, the most important thing to happen to me, ever. She was then known as the prettiest, brightest, nicest girl

David and Mary Shea Dixon's wedding, June 11, 1949.

Dixon as a medalist at the NOCC Golf Invitational with sons (left to right) Stuart, Frank, and Shea, 1957. ()

in Memphis, Tennessee, now known as the prettiest, brightest, nicest girl in New Orleans, Louisiana — actually, the prettiest girl anywhere, and a great wife, mother, and grandmother.

Interestingly, Mary has a unique accomplishment to be proud of. Mary, always an excellent athlete, took up golf when we married, so she was no beginner at the time Arnold Palmer visited our home in 1957. Sitting in our living room, looking out at the New Orleans Country Club golf course, Arnold, Mary, and I decided to stretch our legs and play a few holes. We started at the fifteenth tee. Mary made 3 on a very difficult par-4 . . . and Palmer made 6. Unflappable, she stated at the next tee, "I'm going home to fix dinner for you boys. I've beaten Arnold Palmer by three shots. I'd be out of my mind to continue." In later years as I told the story, I greatly admired my wife's modest comment: "Well," she would say, "after all, it was my home course!"

But back in 1947, I had yet to meet the woman who would become my wife. I was a sectional qualifying medalist for the U.S. Amateur Championship at Pebble Beach, California, rather thrilling for a weekend golfer. I won my first-round match, and then I beat a really good player, John "Sonny" Ellis of Columbus, Georgia, southern intercollegiate champion and captain of a great LSU golf team. My roommate at Pebble Beach was my friend Jay Hebert from Lafayette, a future Ryder Cup star and PGA champion, whom I had nosed out as qualifying medalist from the Louisiana-Mississippi-South Alabama USGA section. Eventually I lost a close match in the third round (thirty-two players) to a top California player whose name now eludes me.

The next year, the U.S. Amateur was to be played at the Memphis Country Club. Living temporarily in Jackson, Mississippi, I was so busy as a sales representative for Great Southern Box Company, my father's old company, then headed by his close friend Shelley Schuster, that I did not try to qualify for the 1948 U.S. Amateur. However, my closest golfing friend, Harry Deas of Jesuit High School and Tulane University, an outstanding player three years older than I, was living in Memphis after a young lifetime in New Orleans. Harry was good enough to have been a much more serious contender than I in any U.S. Amateur championship. A brilliant, gifted young engineer, he could play. We played so well together that we nearly cleaned out many of the top players in Memphis during 1947 and '48, except, of course, two-time U.S. Open champion Cary Middlecoff. Harry and I never messed with him.

Arkansas was part of my sales territory in 1948, which meant traveling through Memphis. Ending a sales trip there on a late Friday evening, I spent the night at Harry and his wife Helen's home. He promptly talked me into gallerying the thirty-six-hole U.S. Amateur final between Willie Turnesa and Ray Billows the next day at the Memphis Country Club.

It was there, walking down the ninth fairway with my great friend, Harry, that I spotted Billy Campbell, later captain of U.S. Walker Cup teams and frequent British and U.S. Amateur champion. I knew Billy, so I went over to say hello. Billy's gallery date that day was Miss Mary Coyle Shea, from a prominent Memphis family and one of the famous Shea sisters, all four gorgeous, intelligent, and very, very nice. Billy Campbell introduced me to Mary. I remember Harry saying to me later, "Wow, Duke [my golf nickname], she's gorgeous."

I thought that through this attractive girl I could meet many other nice girls in Memphis, a city through which I traveled a couple of times a month. I telephoned Mary a couple of days later, asked for a date, and got her earliest open evening—a full two weeks later. Disappointing, but this was to be my Memphis entrée.

For that first date with Mary, in the early fall of 1948, I arrived at her home, a very impressive residence at 233 South Belvedere Boulevard in an upscale area of Memphis. Her father, Dr. John Shea, was a revered, nationally renowned physician. Her brother, Dr. John Shea, Jr., is an international pioneer in inner-ear surgery, married to Lynda Lee Mead, a former Miss America.

Ah, what a reception! Mary's oldest sister, chic Jeanne Leatherman, a stunning, tall beauty with great flair, greeted me. Two other gorgeous sisters, Catharine Roberts and Ellen Thompson, also greeted me, as did Mary's beautiful mother, Mrs. Catharine Shea, a former Democratic national committeewoman, and Mary's grandmother, Mrs. Ellen G. Flanagan.

What an assemblage, all of them terribly impressive to this young New Orleanian's eyes and ears.

Later I realized, or hoped, that I was being "inspected," which would have meant that this incredible girl was at least mildly interested in me. Then came the great moment. Mary, my date for the evening, made a grand entrance, descending an impressive stairway, much the same as the famous actress Loretta Young in her hit TV show. What a sight! Her entrance lacked nothing but the music that night in Memphis. The hot, sweaty, makeup-less girl I had met on the golf course had been transformed into the most impressive young woman I had seen in a young lifetime of inspecting great young beauties. What presence! She walked up to me, tilted my chin, and said, "Oh, yes, I remember you."

It was embarrassing. I was so overwhelmed by the chin tilt that I nearly went to my knees, which would have been so humiliating and laughable that I probably would have been eliminated on the spot from contention for this last of the four great Shea beauties. However, I willingly went to my knees shortly thereafter! I danced that night and others with this incredibly beautiful girl on the Peabody roof in Memphis, the city's prestigious entertainment spot. These details are reasonably accurate, but over the years I admit to embellishing the scene a bit by adding a whiff of Chanel #5, the famous perfume. At any rate I was smitten. We were married nine months later.

Mary Dixon to this day is every bit as impressive as that first evening at South Belvedere in Memphis and on the Peabody roof. There is no doubt in my mind that Governors McKeithen and Edwards, Mayors Morrison, Schiro, and Landrieu—and various media people—began to listen more carefully to this guy wild-talking about NFL and NBA teams, Superdomes, etc., once they saw him with his gorgeous wife, Mary Shea Dixon.

CHAPTER III

Fostering a Dream

It could be said that the New Orleans Saints and the Louisiana Superdome were born on the Tulane University campus on a gorgeous, sunny December afternoon in 1949. It was then that the Tulane University Board met in private session at Tulane University's stately Gibson Hall, facing our city's grand, historic St. Charles Avenue and world-famous Audubon Park with its magnificent oaks and picturesque lagoons—a superb visual setting, New Orleans at its finest.

Those board members and Tulane's president, Dr. Rufus Harris, did not come to praise the mighty Tulane Green Wave for having won their third Southeastern Conference football championship in eleven peacetime years. Instead, they came to examine carefully the university's intercollegiate athletics policies and those of competing institutions. Their ultimate decision was to de-emphasize major intercollegiate athletics at Tulane University, as ordained that day by elimination of degrees in physical education.

When I learned months later of this rather dramatic change in policy, I knew that perennially losing programs in both football and basketball would follow. Predictably, over succeeding years each football weekend in New Orleans became more and more negative and depressing as lopsided losses were piled upon lopsided losses, week after week, for the once mighty Tulane Green Wave, a national power in intercollegiate football from the 1920s until 1950. Tulane's athletics future changed dramatically after that fateful 1949 board meeting.

By 1961, I knew for certain that Tulane's de-emphasis policy was irreversible, and in many ways unfortunate, as a bit of the competitive, joyous spirit seemed to have been squeezed out of our community. Admittedly this might have been just one man's imagination. Nevertheless, I began to think seriously about the National Football League and its enormous possibilities for our region. As part of this process, I wrote down the problems we would face and the assets we possessed for dealing with those problems.

Problems and Assets

Problems
1. Racial segregation laws of Louisiana and every other Southern state, as they existed in 1960.
2. Negative civic attitude in a few isolated quarters.

Assets
1. A great football tradition as already well established in New Orleans.
2. A superb Tulane Stadium, far better than anything then in the NFL. I felt that Tulane Stadium would be available for a New Orleans entry into the National Football League, particularly in view of de-emphasis.

Other Assets
1. Good weather for football.
2. Favorable differences from other Southern cities. New Orleans has always been the South's most moderate city racially.

The more I examined problems and assets, the more optimistic I became about pro football for our city. A cinch, I thought. Little did I know how difficult and time-consuming it would be to bring this cinch to reality.

The first problem on my list was a potentially crippling one. In fact, the issue of segregation had virtually ruined the prestige of the once great Sugar Bowl. Shortly after World War II the Sugar Bowl, often the scene of a mythical college football national championship, replaced the Rose Bowl as the number one New Year's Day bowl game, after the Rose Bowl had concluded contracts to match the far superior Big Ten Champion against the then weak Pacific Coast Conference. But this superiority was short-lived due to racial integration questions. The Orange Bowl concluded a deal with the old Big Eight. Oklahoma and Nebraska loaded up with an avalanche of great young African-American athletes, usually ranking number one or number two nationally, and the Orange Bowl quickly surpassed the lily-white Sugar Bowl in prominence.

Eventually Bear Bryant, the head coach of the University of Alabama, rescued the Sugar Bowl by masterminding a deal with the Southeastern Conference to send its champion to the Sugar Bowl each year. Then came the Civil Rights Act of 1964, which restored the Sugar Bowl to at least equal prestige as the Orange Bowl, usually superior. The "Bear" did his part to end segregation, recruiting young black athletes vigorously, winning several more national championships as a result.

It was in the late 1950s that I came across Gov. Earl K. Long as he walked along Camp Street (amazingly without a state trooper in sight) just outside the old *Times-Picayune* building at Lafayette Square. "I told the Sugar Bowl people that if they would send just one member of their organization to Baton Rouge to ask me to help them with state laws forbidding mixed competition between whites and blacks that I would find a way to do something." In essence that was what Gov. Earl K. Long told me when I stopped him. I was shocked. My opinion of "Uncle Earl" changed considerably, for the better.

Some time later, in considering how to combat the first problem on my list, it dawned on me that a privately owned stadium, such as that owned by Tulane University, should have immunity from state racial segregation laws. After all, a person can invite anyone he or she wants into his or her home. Top lawyers agreed immediately that my private property theory was correct. Besides, I had been encouraged by the Tulane Board, and especially by Joseph Merrick Jones—at that time, 1962, Tulane's board president and New Orleans' unquestioned civic leader—regarding the stadium's availability.

No one to my knowledge has ever posed the question I now ask: If the Sugar Bowl wanted to retain its position as the number one post-season college football game during the late 1950s, they didn't need relief from Governor Long. Nor did they need the 1964 Civil Rights Act. As I discovered with a bit of research sometime during 1960-61, Tulane Stadium, the home of all Sugar Bowl games, was located on private property, and the Sugar Bowl people could have invited whomever they wanted all through the period when the Orange Bowl surpassed them during the late 1950s and early 1960s. Why didn't our Sugar Bowlers take advantage of that fact? The reason, of course, was the very complex and perplexing segregation-integration issues of the time. However, I did not want segregation to prevent either the rise of a future major league franchise or that league's enjoyment by all the city's citizens.

As it turned out they presumably would have taken very little abuse, or none, from the people of our city. When our little group integrated Tulane Stadium in 1963 we ran into very little resistance—maybe two telephone calls; no threats.

Negative civic attitude also was mostly a myth. I was aware of a ridiculous belief that Paul Tulane had stipulated in his will that football could never be played at Tulane on Sundays. Hell, I knew that Paul Tulane died decades before Rutgers and Princeton invented American football.

My one genuine worry was our dominant daily newspaper, the *Times-Picayune.* My parents had taught me years earlier to respect the *Picayune* as well intentioned, but stories about their irascible, sometimes mean-spirited editor filled me with concern, a feeling that was confirmed in future years by countless experiences with "The Editor," George W. Healy, Jr. Here was an opponent to be watched carefully, always. Something of a family friend, he was famous for violent, unpredictable mood changes but was a competent, able newspaperman on his good days. My friend, former mayor Moon Landrieu, was to tell me years later of his experiences with The Editor. Even my dear, sweet mother, then in her early 60s but well attuned to local knowledge, advised me to be ever so careful around the man, advice I followed diligently for twenty difficult years.

My recognition of the city's willingness to embrace a major league sports franchise was confirmed one day in early 1961. Imagine my reaction when the tremendously popular mayor of our city, Chep Morrison, held a news conference announcing that he intended to create a Mayor's Major League Sports Committee and build a new baseball stadium at a site near Lake Pontchartrain so that New Orleans could become a major league sports town.

I knew Chep reasonably well, so I telephoned him immediately to advise that he had the wrong sport and the wrong stadium, pointing out that New Orleans was already a great football town with a superb football stadium that was better by far than anything then in the now booming National Football League, namely Tulane-Sugar Bowl Stadium, with 83,000 excellent seats that I thought could be available under the right circumstances. Right then and there, over the telephone, Chep invited me to become chairman of his new sports committee. I thanked him, stating that his offer was very much appreciated and that I would get back to him within forty-eight hours.

Immediately I called Mr. Clark Salmon, the head of the Bauerlein Agency, at that time the city's most prestigious and successful advertising agency, and asked to see him. I knew Mr. Salmon well, as he was the father of Clark Salmon, Jr., a close friend from my boyhood days. His reply was, "Come on by now, David."

I asked Mr. Salmon's advice about Chep Morrison's invitation, stating that there had to be "dozens" of people more qualified than I for such a position. To my enormous surprise he said almost immediately, "Nonsense, you already are the best man in New Orleans for such a post. You have a million good ideas about sports, plus youth and enthusiasm. And you are your father's son. He was a great man." This was probably the nicest compliment ever paid to me (other than Mary's "I do"). I was flabbergasted and flattered and very, very proud, particularly because of his reference to my late father. I had no idea that anyone of Mr. Salmon's stature had such an opinion of me. All of this was a huge confidence boost.

So, I called Chep Morrison and accepted his invitation. I also told him that I had received an excellent financial offer from someone who wanted to buy Dixon Plywood Corporation and that Mary and I might accept that offer and take a sabbatical with our three sons (Frank, Shea, and Stuart) and go to Europe for the better part of a year. I stated that I could establish contact with the NFL and their commissioner by mail and telephone and an occasional visit to New York from Europe. I had formed Dixon Plywood as a pioneer in the rapidly expanding, prefinished, V-grooved wall paneling industry. Business was booming, but I was fascinated with the NFL potential for our city. Mayor Morrison encouraged me to take that sabbatical but to start working immediately on an NFL franchise.

My close friends Edward Poitevent, (a senior law partner at Jones, Walker, Waechter, Poitevent, Carrere, and Denegre) and New Orleans businessmen Robert "Bobby" Monsted and George "Sonny" Westfeldt came to see my family off for our adventure to Europe, beginning in August 1961. Edward, Bobby, and Sonny agreed strongly with my belief that New Orleans was perfect for an NFL franchise and never wavered in their support in the years ahead. In fact, in 1962, the four of us, along with Bill Helis and Hugh M. Evans, a tremendous person, president of our then leading department store, D. H. Holmes Company, created the New Orleans Pro Football Club, Inc. Evans was a major newspaper advertiser whose mere presence probably kept The Editor at bay. Indeed, I almost blushed in The Editor's presence whenever I said, "Hugh Evans and I believe" at very strategically chosen increments. These officers and stockholders were quite a group, all very, very helpful and influential community leaders. Civic heavy weights, those guys.

In 1962, as our group surveyed the local scene, we knew there were at least six entities that we needed to recognize:

1. Tulane University
2. The people of New Orleans
3. The Sugar Bowl Committee members
4. The African-American community
5. Top local TV and radio stations
6. The dominant local newspaper, the *Times-Picayune*

I knew from the beginning that Tulane's leaders, with only isolated exceptions, would be in our corner, as its key members recognized immediately the economic value to our city of a

National Football League franchise. Joseph Merrick Jones had assured me sometime during 1961 and again early in 1962, in his position as president of Tulane's Board of Administrators, that we would have his full support for the use of Tulane-Sugar Bowl Stadium for an NFL franchise, saying: "Look, an NFL franchise would be a great thing for our city. So I think Tulane University has to take the same position as Engine Charlie Wilson, chairman of General Motors, who once stated, 'If it's good for our country, it has to be good for GM and hopefully vice versa.' So if the NFL is good for New Orleans, it will be good for Tulane, hopefully vice versa at all times. Tulane will be good citizens," he said. I was impressed with the scope of his view.

Joe Jones was a great leader, and his loss to our city during a tragic fire late in 1962 was a community disaster. After my initial shock over his death, I feared that we had lost the opportunity to use Tulane Stadium in our NFL bid. To my relief, within the week, Darwin Fenner, who succeeded Mr. Jones as president of Tulane's board, telephoned to assure me of the availability of Tulane Stadium to the group Edward, Bobby, and I had formed.

Too, the people of New Orleans, we felt, would be strongly supportive. Our main focus was football, and New Orleans has always been a great football town, thanks to early Tulane powerhouses prior to de-emphasis and the Sugar Bowl. New Orleanians had a chance to prove that support when the Pro Football Club learned that my friend Jack De Fee, a civic-minded New Orleanian, was planning a preseason American Football League (AFL) game at City Park Stadium for August 1962, featuring Billy Cannon, the LSU national championship team's great running back of 1958 and 1959. I immediately contacted Jack, and I agreed to participate in promoting the game to help with its success, billing it as "New Orleans' first step toward an NFL or AFL franchise." An overflow crowd of 31,000 in a 26,000-seat stadium was the result. That evening we received more than 20,000 informal season ticket pledges for a future pro football franchise. Incredibly, most actually bought season tickets for the Saints in 1967.

In our march toward major league pro football, we found the Sugar Bowlers to be wonderfully cooperative, and the African-American community was ecstatic, particularly when I informed them of the private property concept and our absolute intent to sell tickets first-come, first-served for the first time in the history of the Old South.

We were tremendously pleased with the outstanding support and progressive attitude of all the top TV and radio companies of our Gulf South area, all of whom I courted almost daily. But, oh boy, I still worried every day in the 1960s all the way through the 1970s about the *Picayune* and The Editor, and with good reason. All of us worried about the *Times-Picayune,* which in those days had the reputation among its strongest critics of being professional progress blockers. They had been negative from the beginning, even about the Sugar Bowl, their sports editor stating about 1933 in a memorable column (one that I read as a ten-year-old) that "our streets are too narrow for a New Year's Day football game." Besides, as mentioned earlier, the *Picayune*'s editor-in-chief, the infamous Editor, carried the reputation of being irascible and negative, perhaps even mean and vindictive under certain circumstances, at a time when our city needed an enlightened, progressive editorial voice of sanity and moderation. My associates and I knew that we would have to drag The Editor kicking and screaming into the twentieth century. Nevertheless, no one could label even the "old" *Picayune* as "racist." That sort of demagoguery has never been well received in New Orleans, no matter the political spin spread nationwide during Katrina by misguided national news media and federal officials covering their *derrieres.* Even so, the *Times-Picayune* of the early 1960s was certainly not the *Times-Picayune* of today, with Ashton Phelps, Jr., as publisher and Jim Amoss as editor, both civic-minded, very progressive thinkers. Indeed, their newspaper today is among the very best dailies in America.

However, when we were introducing New Orleans to the National Football League through the sponsorship of a series of preseason games beginning in 1963, The Editor gave orders to the *Picayune*'s sports department staff that they could write about the NFL only on an every-other-day basis, as admitted by

Buddy Diliberto, the paper's daily sports columnist and Bob Roesler, their sports editor. On the week of a big, unprecedented NFL doubleheader in 1963 nothing was scheduled to be written in the paper on Monday, Wednesday, or Friday. I solved that one by buying expensive, full-page ads. Now I was a customer and coverage problems disappeared.

Buddy himself was always a proponent of the NFL, very consistent in his support, but even he during these early years carried a bit of *Picayune* negativism with him, unnecessarily insisting that attendance at preseason games was not a harbinger of a franchise-to-come. We never once advertised or featured such a premise. I simply pointed out in hundreds of civic club speeches over the years that if we drew poorly for our preseason games of 1963 through 1956 the NFL almost certainly would ask, "Where's the interest?" The sports editor, Bob Roesler, an outstanding human being, was in my opinion somewhat inhibited, or intimidated early on by the *Picayune*'s negativism and The Editor. Initially 75 percent supportive, 25 percent lukewarm, Bob quickly became 100 percent supportive.

Today, the *Picayune*'s position toward the Saints is everything that a great newspaper should be: fair in every respect. They present both sides in a constructive manner. One of many positive positions taken by today's *Times-Picayune* was their critical support of building the New Orleans Arena. Without that arena we would not have the NBA's Hornets or the arena football team, the Voodoo.

An NFL Doubleheader, 1963

With the availability of Tulane Stadium confirmed, we studied steps that might lead us to obtaining a franchise. From frequent travels to NFL meetings and visits with league commissioner Pete Rozelle in New York, I learned that the New Orleans Pro Football Club should sponsor some NFL preseason games, utilizing Tulane Stadium. We planned very carefully to make certain that our first adventure would tie into our franchise efforts. So, for effect, we conceived a football doubleheader, carefully matching the Dallas Cowboys against the Detroit Lions and the Chicago Bears against the Baltimore Colts. This was only the second football doubleheader in history, the first having been produced by Art Modell, then the owner of the Cleveland Browns.

We knew that Tulane University was the beneficiary of large grants from the Ford Foundation, so our first strategy was to go after the Detroit Lions, owned by William Clay Ford, son of Edsel Ford, Henry Ford's only son and a first-class person in every respect. Bill Ford's brother was Henry Ford II, chairman of Ford Motor Company. We contacted Edwin Anderson, president and general manager of the Detroit Lions. Mr. Anderson said in his club's formal acceptance that the Lions would "be honored to come to New Orleans and famous old Tulane Stadium to participate in your spectacular NFL doubleheader."

Eddie Anderson and I became good friends, and I asked him if I would be out of line to suggest that Bill Ford make the formal request of Tulane for the use of the stadium. Eddie replied, "Absolutely not, compose the letter, and I'll present it to Mr. Ford." I did compose that letter (with a strategic reference to the Ford Foundation) and, sure enough, Billy Ford signed it exactly as written after transferring it to his Ford Motor Company letterhead. Later, Tulane authorities and their president, Dr. Herbert Longenecker, told me how pleased they were to receive such a "nice letter from such a prominent member of the Ford family." I never told a soul who was the real letter writer — except under great pressure from my friend Edward Poitevent, who had suspected me almost immediately. "Recognized my style," he said.

Tex Schramm of the expansion Dallas Cowboys was commissioner Pete Rozelle's close friend, adviser, and confidant. Indeed, Pete was planning to be present at our big event, so we matched the expansion Cowboys against the Lions and Mr. Ford.

To book the teams for the second game, we employed a different approach. It was understood that the real power of the National Football League in 1963 was still Mr. George Halas, the league's founder and patriarch. In a stroke of genius Hugh

Evans spoke up: "David, you should fly to Chicago to invite Mr. Halas in person. And be sure to take your gorgeous wife with you. Mary Dixon will make such a great impression that Papa Bear might actually help you get the Baltimore Colts and Johnny Unitas." So, Mary and I flew to Chicago to invite Mr. Halas in person. He was delighted and said to our astonishment, that he would get us the Baltimore Colts and Johnny Unitas, which he did by telephone as we sat in his office. The Colts even changed a date to accommodate Mr. Halas. Yes, he was the power of the NFL, and Mary Dixon had somehow woven her magic spell again. From that moment on I regarded my friend and mentor, Hugh Evans, as a prophet.

At that point we had Mr. Ford's Detroit Lions against Pete Rozelle's great friend's Dallas Cowboys, with a second game to follow for a grand, unprecedented 1963 NFL doubleheader featuring George "Papa Bear" Halas's Chicago Bears against Johnny Unitas's Baltimore Colts, owned by Carroll Rosenbloom, another NFL power and chairman of the NFL's Expansion Committee. An excellent, politically selected group, if I do say so myself. We hoped that New Orleans now had strong supporters within the NFL. I knew that we did. The New Orleans Pro Football Club was off to an excellent start.

Alleluia

The year of our doubleheader was 1963, well before Hale Boggs became one of the few Southerners to vote for the Voting Rights Act of 1965, an act of great courage by a great man. Louisiana still had all kinds of racial laws on its books, even if more lenient by a good bit for "people of color" than other Southern states. We were proud of the fact that New Orleans has always been a "different" city, light years ahead of other Southern cities (and many Northern cities as well) in race relations and good will.

Our 1963 doubleheader would be played at Tulane Stadium, private property owned by Tulane University, which meant that we could sell tickets on private property without regard to such laws. I told Tulane officials before the 1963 doubleheader of the private property situation and that we wanted to be the first Southern city to sell first come, first served football tickets, three years before Atlanta or anyone in the South. I talked privately to Mr. Darwin Fenner, the president of Tulane's board, informing him that this policy was our strong preference, and God bless him, he replied that Tulane University would have it no other way. To say the least, Commissioner Rozelle was very interested in what we were doing.

When we put tickets on sale for our big doubleheader, I carefully instructed all personnel at the Tulane ticket office how to advise patrons of ticket availability. We prepared a giant chart showing all sold tickets, asking the young ladies selling the tickets to say, "Any unmarked seat is available. Everything is first come, first served."

Finally, two weeks later our first African-American football fan visited the Tulane ticket office. I watched this historic ticket-selling drama from six feet away—the first desegregated sports event in the history of the Old South—and our young lady handled the situation perfectly. She showed the ticket chart, and then stated the words, "first come, first served."

At that moment our visitor asked, "You mean I can sit anywhere I want?"

Our young lady answered affirmatively, at which point our "colored" football fan mumbled, almost under his breath, "Alleluia!"

It has always embarrassed me as a man that I weep easily. That day I had to turn away as tears came to my eyes when I realized that—at this instant at least—one little injustice and indignity was being removed from this gentleman's life forever. It was a poignant moment. I was touched by the dignified manner of this nice gentleman and by the significance of the act. As long as I live I shall never forget that scene at the Tulane ticket office on Willow Street. When I related this incident to my partners in the New Orleans Pro Football Club, Hugh Evans spoke up immediately, "We're doing the right thing for our city. Well done, David."

I shall never forget, either, a telephone call from Allen Favrot, a friend, who began the conversation with, "David, I under-stand you are integrating Tulane Stadium," which shook me a bit. Then he continued, "Congratulations. I admire what you're doing." Allen Favrot is a distinguished New Orleanian from a family of distinguished New Orleanians. He bought twelve tick-ets in Section GG. I was proud of my friend.

We did have one game-night misfortune. During the third quarter of game one (Detroit-Dallas), it rained as hard as I have seen for twenty-eight minutes, with lots of thunder and absolutely terrifying lightning. The field flooded, and we had to suspend play for approximately two hours. Almost everyone, thousands of people, sought refuge under the stadium. Fearing a race riot or some similar act of unrest under these conditions, I hurried to the ramps, but as I entered the rain-protected area I was momentarily amazed to see everyone laughing and throw-ing buckets of water on and at each other, having loads of fun despite the flooding caused by what the newspapers reported as "almost solid water." Within two weeks of that enormous rain-storm, the Beauticians Association of New Orleans named me their Man of the Year for "creating $100,000 worth of ruined hair-dos!" That rainstorm scared the hell out of me, but it put a big, broad smile on the faces of beauticians for miles around.

Later I realized that I didn't really expect a race riot that night. The good-natured throwing of water balloons, the riotous laughing, those were the things I expected of our New Orleanians. I was and am very, very proud of our city. Generally speaking, New Orleanians are nicer to each other (and to visitors) than people any place else I have been. Many New Orleanians believe that ours is a city with a soul. It appeared that our four important NFL owners—Halas, Ford, Murchison, and Rosenbloom—agreed, or so we hoped.

Eventually, the flooded field drained, and the Chicago Bears and Baltimore Colts finished game two at 1:00 A.M. Sunday. The great Mr. George "Papa Bear" Halas had told me, "Don't worry, David, the Chicago Bears will play until 4:00 A.M. if necessary!" No wonder he was so revered. Thanks to Mr. Halas, our double-header actually was a huge success, and the idea for the Superdome was born on that stormy evening.

Dixon at the 1963 NFL doubleheader held at Tulane Stadium.

Overall the 1963 doubleheader was a huge success, drawing more than 50,000 people on a hot, humid, rainy August evening at eight dollars each, the highest priced football ticket at that time in America for mere exhibition games ("preseason" games, as Commissioner Pete Rozelle taught us to say). We were off and running toward the NFL and major league sports for our great city.

Which Pocket Has the $2,000?

Even though we had been in a good, secure legal position for our blockbuster 1963 doubleheader, I wanted to relieve Tulane of any future embarrassment or unfortunate incident related to the integrated seating at the game. The university's board had been magnificent, but I wanted to cover every base for them and our city. After passage of the Civil Rights Act of 1964, following a little investigation and legal research, my associates and I were advised by attorneys that the Louisiana bans on mixed seating, breathing the same stadium air, mixed competition, etc., were now regarded by federal courts as clearly unconstitutional. Our hope was that they could be struck down quietly, no headlines, in federal court in New Orleans.

I thought this could be arranged with good luck and some smarts. I also decided that we should not ask a white lawyer to undertake this task, as these were still touchy times in America, even in New Orleans. Therefore, I asked David Kleck, our advisor on racial matters, to arrange a meeting for me, and me alone, with the black power structure of our area. The meeting would take place at historic Old St. Peter Claver Hall on Orleans Avenue, an African-American community center.

I went alone that appointed evening. I was very well received by everyone, which was wonderful because I was nervous and quite apprehensive. I relaxed very quickly, thanks to my new friends. I simply wanted to get New Orleans into the National Football League, and I knew that certain outdated, outmoded Louisiana laws had to be struck from the books, the sooner the better for the city. Also, it would benefit the Sugar Bowl organization, playing on a fast-changing national scene.

I asked these very able, dedicated gentlemen to assign one of their staff lawyers to go before the federal bench and do our work for us. I was told very quickly that everyone admired our goals and sympathized with what we were doing, but they had only three lawyers with federal court experience, and they were "snowed under."

When I asked what could be done to accelerate our agenda, the committee's leader laughed sympathetically, looked around at his associates, laughed again, then eventually said, "Money." Everyone else, including myself, also laughed, and the tension lifted quickly, so I asked, "How much money?"

The group of perhaps twenty community leaders asked me to step into a little private waiting room so that they could discuss that question. I excused myself, and within a few minutes they invited me to rejoin them, saying, "How does $2,000 sound?" I told them promptly that $2,000 sounded pretty high to me, but I asked, "May I go back to the reception area and think about it for a minute or two?"

Well, I had expected at least $3,000 or $4,000, so I had $6,000 cash in my pocket. I quickly sorted out $2,000 into my right front pocket, with $4,000 tucked into my left. A first-rate melodrama causing much anxiety, but history was on the other side of that door . . . and I knew it! These were personal funds, because I did not want any possible exposure for Poitevent, Monsted, Evans, Westfeldt, and Helis or for Tulane University. Cash, no checks.

As I reentered the meeting room, a terrible thought hit me, "Which the hell pocket has the $2,000 and which has the $4,000?" I momentarily sweated buckets, but I guessed correctly and paid the $2,000 cash on the spot. To my utter amazement I received an impromptu standing ovation, which touched me deeply. Their leader and I hugged. Another ovation. I felt pretty good about humanity.

The laws were struck down by summary court judgment, as predicted, without fanfare or publicity. The young lawyer handling the matter was Dutch Morial, destined to become mayor of New Orleans. A terrific, confident, cocky-in-a-healthy-way young man. Dutch did a nice job. The case was cited by lawyers for other Southern states as precedent for knocking out similar laws by summary court judgment. We were pleased to be rid of those old, punitive laws that ultimately would have been a hindrance to our NFL aspirations for our city and state.

Inexplicably, that magnificent, historic old building, St. Peter Claver Hall, an Orleans Avenue architectural gem, was later demolished and replaced with an unimpressive little "modern" structure that is not worthy of the heroic, sainted priest, Peter Claver, an early pioneer in the field of social progress for African-Americans. I wonder who was responsible for that little tragedy.

Naïvely, I had no idea of the time pitfalls, backbreaking work, and considerable expense that lay ahead of us before the New Orleans Saints in 1967 would line up before a sellout crowd of 83,000 at Tulane Stadium.

CHAPTER IV

Gathering Support from the NFL

The Lamar Hunt Opportunity

Having proven that New Orleans could successfully host NFL games—and to a racially mixed crowd, no less—my associates and I set about finding an individual owner for a New Orleans franchise. From the vantage points and perceptions of the early twenty-first century, New Orleanians and Louisianians can look back with regret at the incredible ineptness and disappointments of the John Mecom, Jr. years, 1967-85, and the off and on misfortunes of the ongoing Tom Benson era, including the sad illness and death of the great Jim Finks, the departure of the talented and mostly successful Jim Mora, the terrible misadventure of the Mike Ditka years, and today's seemingly endless, tedious "negotiations" by owner Tom Benson and the Superdome Commission (the State of Louisiana).

Today it seems almost impossible that my associates and I passed on a de facto opportunity to bring to New Orleans in 1963 Lamar Hunt and his AFL championship team and eventual NFL Super Bowl champions, the Dallas Texans of 1960-62, known to all since 1963 as the Kansas City Chiefs. Lamar Hunt, who passed away in December 2006, was the founder and the prime organizer of the old American Football League that eventually merged with the NFL to become today's monumentally successful National Football League. Hunt realized during the 1962 season that two competing teams in the Dallas market was one too many. Either his Dallas Texans or Clint Murchison and Tex Schramm's Dallas Cowboys had to go. Neither was drawing even high-school-size crowds.

I made it my business to cultivate both sides, spending many hours with Lamar and his Texans and with Pete Rozelle's close friend, Tex Schramm, and his wife, Marti, with whom Mary became quite friendly. Mary and I were particularly impressed with Lamar, at that time almost painfully quiet and reserved but obviously a very, very good person. It seemed that almost every weekend during the football season we were in Dallas to watch either the Texans or the Cowboys and to socialize with both groups, even traveling with the Texans to many of their games. We did the same thing many years later with the New Orleans Breakers of the United States Football League. Ironically, to this day I've never ridden a charter for the Saints, the NFL franchise I founded and named after hundreds of thousands of dollars of expense and thousands of man hours of hard work. Besides, at my age you can't beat TV and the comforts of home and a good wife's company.

Here's where my associates and I made a regrettable error in judgment. Lamar was ready to move his team out of Dallas, and we had done a good job of selling him on New Orleans as a prospective AFL expansion city, so he was interested in moving to our city, particularly if Tulane Stadium were available. At some point in time, probably immediately following the 1962 season, Lamar went so far as to bring his very capable business manager, Jack Steadman, to New Orleans to work out a deal for me to become president, general manager, or a similar position at a flattering salary with 2 percent ownership in the team at no cost to me, provided a satisfactory stadium deal could be arranged at Tulane. Lamar, of course, would be chairman/CEO. He and I met quietly and privately with a select committee from the Tulane Board of Administrators. Lamar was so concerned about secrecy and security that he asked me to tell the committee that his request for stadium availability was for *any* AFL franchise.

The select Tulane committee was chaired by my good friend Lester Lautenschlaeger, captain and quarterback of the undefeated Tulane team of 1925, and a former co-head coach at Tulane, 1932-35, with Ted Cox. Lester was a keen student of the game, a handsome, trim, and well-spoken person, a true gentleman. I think that Lester was mildly anti pro football, but he was a good chairman of the committee that met with us. In fairness, I would say that nothing was worked out with Mr. Hunt because neither Lester nor I could get Lamar to say that he was interested in the use of Tulane Stadium for *himself*, for his Dallas Texans to move to New Orleans and become our city's franchise. I seem to recall also that the word was that the Tulane board favored the NFL, naturally, as did my associates, which contributed to my own attitude of the moment.

Just weeks later, I realized that I had blown a great opportunity for our city—and perhaps for myself and for Tulane University—because at that point in time my own preference, and particularly that of our community and media, was for the NFL and local ownership. However, my choice from a personal standpoint by far was Lamar Hunt, a first-class person in every way. I have enormous respect for Lamar and his wife, Norma, to this moment.

I should have realized the full significance of the fact that Lamar was a favored son of oil tycoon H. L. Hunt, the patriarch of what at that time might have been one of the richest families in the world. It should have been obvious to me that the AFL would survive because of that wealth and power and probably merge with the NFL. Though I believed in this possibility, it was not a certainty. Rumors of AFL weakness were almost rampant; one key *Picayune* writer referred to the AFL as a "Mickey Mouse League" on a regular basis. In truth, the Tulane board, comprised of seasoned business leaders, should have recognized the huge opportunity at hand. All of us blew this one, but the primary blame is mine. I knew it then, I know it now, and it will haunt me forever, not for myself but for New Orleans, our city.

Lamar eventually moved his team to Kansas City in the spring of 1963, where he has invested millions of dollars, created a Super Bowl championship team, and is respected as a great citizen. He is an able, superb leader in his quiet, effective way.

By comparison, young John Mecom, Jr., original owner of the New Orleans Saints, gave us years and years of losing seasons and disappointments, and had little or no involvement in the civic and social affairs of our community. Rightly or wrongly,

John was considered a playboy by New Orleanians.

Here's what I should have done. I knew Darwin Fenner, the president of the Tulane Board of Administrators, reasonably well. Had I visited privately with Darwin, I am certain I could have convinced him that the solution would have been for Tulane to make a confidential, unpublicized commitment to the American Football League, subject only to a condition that the board must approve any individual owner, a perfectly reasonable stipulation that also would have preserved Lamar's understandable desire for security and confidentiality. Tulane would reserve an NFL possibility until the Texans could become contracted to Tulane Stadium. This plan is so terribly simple that to this day I remain embarrassed that I did not think of it at the time. A nitwit should have thought of that stratagem. This nitwit did not. I knew that Lamar would have moved his team to New Orleans within two weeks of an agreement with Tulane.

As proof of Lamar Hunt's genuine interest in New Orleans, he did ask me after the Tulane meeting to obtain approval from City Park's Board of Governors as to the availability of City Park Stadium, their ultimate such resolution sitting somewhere in my files at this very moment. In the final analysis City Park Stadium was and is not a major facility, nor could it have been upgraded sufficiently. I would not have let Lamar move there. It has served the community extremely well as a high-school football stadium and even as an Olympic Trials track and field facility, but Tulane's occasional football use of City Park Stadium is a mistake and dreadful for recruiting.

Lamar Hunt is in my opinion the best sports franchise owner in the world. With Lamar Hunt as owner of the New Orleans Saints, there would have been no John Mecom, Jr., no Tom Benson. I cannot believe I blew that one! I realize now that I lacked top-level business sophistication and experience at that point in time, and, consequently, the self-confidence necessary to take charge.

One factor probably was Mayor Chep Morrison's resignation to become ambassador to the Organization of the American States and, finally, his tragic death in a plane crash. Chep, I think, would have seized an opportunity for a Lamar Hunt tie-in. He would have said, "I can sell this guy to Tulane and to the football fans of New Orleans easily! A piece of cake!" I did not possess such self-confidence at that time, even though Mayor Vic Schiro had continued with me as his major league sports chairman.

The only thing I can say in defense of myself is that we did eventually create our New Orleans Saints and our Louisiana Superdome. Besides, we were blessed for a while with Jim Finks' presence, a person much the quality of Lamar Hunt.

Regardless of what might have been with Lamar Hunt, I look at "what is." And I wish Tom Benson the best of everything. I regard Benson as a rough, gruff person whose major flaws include a misguided sense of top-level public relations and, of course, his lack of basic football knowledge, which has cost him very dearly on more than one occasion. As I look back at the Lamar Hunt misadventure, I realize that our group believed strongly that New Orleans, equipped with Tulane Stadium, would get an NFL franchise, superior by far to the AFL of 1963. Even so, I blew it. Imagine Lamar Hunt as owner of the New Orleans Saints! Lamar Hunt, the best owner in all of sports, not just football, instead of our great city's sad experiences of the past forty years.

Clearing and Cooler by Game Time

I had made it my business to cultivate Pete Rozelle, the young NFL commissioner who had succeeded the great Bert Bell. Pete had been the highly successful general manager of the old Los Angeles Rams (formerly the Cleveland Rams) and in the mid-1960s was relatively new in his role as commissioner and understandably very conservative and careful in every move he made. His hesitancy at this time reflected a general feeling amongst team owners. At an early date NFL owners were concerned about competition from the new upstart American Football League and the antitrust suit that NFL attorneys felt was inevitable. Consequently, "expansion" had become a dirty word, and I knew that we had a long period of waiting ahead of us—but perhaps not if we joined the AFL. Having foolishly

passed on Lamar Hunt and his Dallas Texans in 1962, in 1963-64
I recommended several strategies to my associates. First, we
would continue to sponsor preseason games at Tulane Stadium,
making friends among NFL owners and management. Mary
and I would attend all NFL league meetings, which were
attended by many wives. I knew that Mary would make great
new friends for us. Sure enough she succeeded, becoming daily
communicants at mass with Jim Finks of the Vikings, several of
the Halases of the Bears, the Rooneys of the Steelers, and the
Maras of the Giants. Attendees from our city proudly wore New
Orleans Saints badges I had ordered, and our great new friends
and fabulous supporters, Buddy Diliberto and Peter Finney,
originally of the *New Orleans States-Item* and later a top columnist at the *Picayune,* were now able to be present at the NFL
league meetings. Perhaps even The Editor was beginning to
sense progress. I enjoyed those associations immensely. And we
quietly, very quietly, visited with AFL people and their commissioner, Joe Foss, the much-decorated Marine Corps ace fighter
pilot of World War II.

In our bid to win over the NFL, we found one very strong
supporter in Vince Lombardi. Vince did not let the spectacular
success of our 1963 doubleheader go unnoticed. He actually
called *me* about playing a preseason game for us in 1964 against
the old St. Louis Cardinals (the football team formerly known as
the Chicago Cardinals), owned by the late Charles Bidwill's
sons, Stormy and Billy. There was one incredibly amusing
moment that clinched Lombardi's support for NFL expansion
into New Orleans.

The 1963 torrential rain during our unprecedented doubleheader became almost legendary, a fixture in the minds of many
New Orleanians, and a potential problem for us for future preseason attendance and, consequently, for an eventual franchise.
So, I took my good friend Al Wester to lunch one day in July
1964 and pitched an idea to him.

Al Wester had become famous for national broadcasts of Notre
Dame football. My idea was that on game day we would run
taped weather forecasts something like this: "Hello, football fans,
this is Al Wester with your up-to-the-minute weather forecast for

tonight's big game at Tulane Stadium between Vince Lombardi's mighty Green Bay Packers with LSU's All Pro Jimmy Taylor versus the exciting St. Louis Cardinals. Clearing and cooler by game time, perfect conditions, kickoff 8:00 P.M. Tickets on sale at D.H. Holmes, Maison Blanche, and Tulane Stadium."

Unfortunately, Al was going to be out of town for the August 1964 weekend of Green Bay versus St. Louis and unavailable to do the game-day weather forecast radio spots. Instead, Al and WWL's meteorologist agreed to tape the commercials ahead of time. Even though we were taping this "up to the minute forecast" in July for an August date, I pointed out to Al that this was a night game and certainly it would be cooler at night than during the day. I also reminded him that a typical summer day in New Orleans was afternoon showers, clearing during early evening. So, "clearing and cooler by game time" was an excellent possibility. I promised Al and WWL Radio that the spots would be canceled if a hurricane or other big storm system headed our way. WWL Radio, owned then by Loyola University, which later bestowed on me an honorary degree, Doctor of Humane Letters (whatever that is), wanted pro football for our city as much as we did.

When game day arrived the Packers were staying at the Airport Hilton near their chartered flight, so I paid a courtesy welcome call on Coach Lombardi. He was relaxed and very gracious, and we swapped stories back and forth. He was quite a guy, with a wonderful New York accent and a gravelly voice, this one-time member of Fordham's great Seven Blocks of Granite. In Vince Lombardi's playing days Fordham was a college power.

It was a drizzly day, with gray, menacing clouds everywhere, no hint of sunshine, and sort of a misty rain. Coach Lombardi noticed my worried glances toward the picture window in his hotel suite and said, "Oh, don't worry about the weather. Just before you came I heard a forecast for perfect weather for tonight."

I'd forgotten for a split second about the Al Wester commercials, so I momentarily rejoiced, then started worrying again as

I recalled the wording. I asked Vince where he had heard such a forecast, and he said, "Oh, on the radio. That guy who does the Notre Dame games, Al something or other."

With that, I decided to tell Vince the whole story, and to my great relief he almost fell out of his chair laughing. I joined in the laughter, a little uneasily, an experience sort of like laughing with Professor Marcoux at Tulane as a sixteen-year-old freshman. Finally, he patted me on the knee and said, "Dave, anybody with such a vivid imagination deserves our support. New Orleans will get Green Bay's vote. Don't worry about it. And we'll bring our rain cleats for tonight. We always do, just in case."

We lucked out: no rain, good weather, great crowd. Sure enough, the weather was "clearing and cooler by game time." I knew it all along; the record shows that I actually predicted it.

Green Bay won 20 to 7 before a crowd of 75,229, easily the biggest preseason crowd for that year anywhere and to this day the biggest in history for a non-league city. Buddy de Monsabert, the Tulane ticket manager, told me that game-day sales were "far and away" the biggest he had ever seen, or heard about, anywhere.

Two years later we got Green Bay's expansion vote.

"Clearing and cooler by game time" has become almost a slogan in the Dixon household about various situations. In fact, it is a part of our family vernacular to cover almost any potentially negative circumstance. We laugh, but not as hard as Vince Lombardi did.

After the game, I asked Coach Lombardi what time their plane was leaving that night. "Oh, we're not going back tonight. I'm giving our guys a night on the town. Most of our players have heard about New Orleans all of their lives but have never been here. It's a special city, you know."

Vince Lombardi knew where and when to give his guys a bit of relaxation, a night on the town, in what we believe is the best city in America. Hell, I know now, Coach Lombardi, wherever you are, that New Orleans is indeed a "special" city. I've always had that feeling about my hometown. During that visit to New Orleans, Vince met my wife. He said to me later, "Dave, that wife of yours automatically makes you an impressive guy." A nice compliment for my gorgeous wife, but her biggest compliment was still to come from Donald Trump.

In August 1964, I was pretty certain that New Orleans and Atlanta would be the fifteenth and sixteenth cities in the NFL. But when?

Buddy Young at Antoine's

Though we were steadily gaining support from within the NFL, and New Orleans had attracted the favor of the likes of Vince Lombardi and Lamar Hunt, the city still had to prove itself. Pete Rozelle, the commissioner of the National Football League, sent one of his key assistants, Buddy Young, to New Orleans to check us out "racially." I recognized that this action by the NFL commissioner almost certainly meant that we were on our way into the National Football League.

I knew my city. At the same time, I knew Buddy Young well and regarded him as a super person, no trouble-maker. I trusted everything would work out during Buddy Young's visit, but nevertheless I was anxious. Plenty anxious. This was early 1965, and not too much had changed in New Orleans, as in other Southern cities, after the passage of the Civil Rights Act of 1964, a giant step forward in our nation's history. Most of our top restaurants in mid-1965 were still lily white in their main dining rooms, although it could be said that slowly, slowly progress was being made. For example, whenever our top community white leaders wanted to meet semi-socially with their African-American counterparts or vice versa, it was done in private rooms of Antoine's and other upscale restaurants or hotels. *But at least they were meeting.* Also, many community leaders were entertaining racially mixed groups at home, perhaps far more frequently and earlier than in other cities. Mary and I had been guests at such events. Hotels were "open." Though change was slow in our city, it was advancing much quicker, I maintain, than in any other Southern city, including Atlanta.

Thus, I welcomed Buddy Young's visit. At that moment

Antoine's, then unquestionably our top restaurant in quality and clientele, was still in the private rooms stage when hosting a group of whites and blacks. I would have been delighted to hold a nice dinner party at our home for Buddy, but instinct told me that I had to go further. So I called Antoine's famous and always pleasant proprietor, Mr. Roy Alciatore, and told him my story. "There can be no back rooms. If you turn me down, I'll simply go elsewhere with never a word to anyone, but I far prefer Antoine's. What do you say?" Roy Alciatore said, "I say let's get it done. You and Buddy Young will be most welcome." He added, "I'm proud of you, David." Hell, I was proud of Roy, not the reverse.

On the fateful night at Antoine's we were greeted quietly and matter-of-factly and seated right in the middle of their main dining room. We received no stares. There I was, quietly integrating our city's most famous restaurant. At least half a dozen friends stopped at our table, and I introduced Buddy Young as "my friend" and as "the former All Pro star of the famous old Baltimore Colts and great All-American tailback, who won two Rose Bowls for the University of Illinois, now a chief assistant to Commissioner Pete Rozelle of the NFL." Actually, Buddy Young, an enormously likable person, was still a household name in those days, so no embellishments were necessary.

Things were going swimmingly, until I glanced over Buddy's right shoulder and caught the eye of a somewhat older family friend who had moved here from a Northern city. He was very, very socially accepted, with a high-society, very attractive debutante daughter. He was the picture of an urbane, sophisticated business leader-socialite. Unfortunately, this was a person I knew to be the closest thing to a Ku Kluxer in genteel, polite society anywhere. A "tough mother," as we say in New Orleans, a white supremacist. This "family friend" seemed to be glowering at me. Finally, still glowering, he rose slowly from his table and started walking toward ours. I was seriously ill—as distracted and distressed as I have ever been—at the thought that he was going to create a scene.

I moved to introduce Buddy when he quickly stuck out his hand to him and said, "You're Buddy Young, aren't you? I'm so and so, a past president of the University of Illinois Alumni Association, and I just want to thank you in person for what you have done for our university. Welcome to our city." He added, "Especially for those three touchdowns against Michigan." I knew that everyone in the Big Ten hated Michigan simply because they won so much, and my glowering friend was no exception. All went well, but was I ever glad to see him walk back to his own table!

Now, Buddy was no fool, and he must have seen in my face the emotional distress I was experiencing. Somewhat laughingly, he commented on my discomfort. I knew instinctively that I could level with Buddy, so with great relief and much amusement, I explained, concluding with "So thank God you made all those touchdown runs against Michigan." With that Buddy broke up, laughing so hard that I knew we had become good, close friends who had just shared what could be called a historic experience, the peaceful integration of a New Orleans landmark.

This was definitely the case, as I learned from Pete Rozelle a few weeks later when he told me that Buddy Young had convinced him New Orleans would pass any racial test with flying colors. I already knew that fact about our city and its people, but it was extremely gratifying to hear it from Pete and to know that Buddy had endorsed us.

I am pleased and honored that the New Orleans Saints and the Louisiana Superdome led me to the unlikely opportunities of integrating major spectator events in our state and of breaking color lines at restaurants in our city. I never doubted New Orleans, but that idiot from Chicago scared the hell out of me!

Even so, the mere fact that Pete Rozelle was checking us out told me that we probably were not much more than one year away from the NFL franchise we had sought since 1960. I confided this information only to my wife and our governor, who agreed that my hunch was probably correct. And, of course, I told Sonny Westfeldt, Edward Poitevent, Hugh Evans, and Robert Monsted, four great supporters who had been stalwarts from the beginning. They broke up laughing at my description of "Dinner at Antoine's."

It would have been nice if I also could have shared this feeling with The Editor, but my every instinct warned me away. My wife and our governor agreed that my hunch was probably correct. So did my mother, who knew The Editor fairly well. Somehow or other I actually liked The Editor, maybe because it was such fun beating him at every turn. He definitely added zest to my life.

CHAPTER V

The New Orleans Saints

Nine Plus Fifteen Equals Twenty-Four
(A Football Equation)

Mary always liked the late Pete Rozelle, who said on several public occasions that "without the efforts of Mary and Dave Dixon, there would have been no New Orleans Saints." People often refer to me, erroneously, as "the father of the Louisiana Superdome," almost always introducing me in that manner. Sure, I dreamed up the idea, the concept, some of its design features, its uses, and I sold it to our governor and to the people of Louisiana, but the real father of the Superdome was John McKeithen. Without him there would have been no Superdome, period. It was easy for me to cheer him on. He risked his political skin as costs rose and other problems emerged, but the governor never wavered, pulling one rabbit after another out of the hat.

I must describe also the last-minute heroics, effort, and assistance provided by Hale Boggs while he was House majority whip. There was no retiring as a multimillionaire lobbyist for that Louisianian, nor would there ever have been such a career for Hale Boggs. Lindy, his wife, is of the same stripe. He delivered critical, decisive support to help us bring about the New Orleans Saints and the Louisiana Superdome. It's a wonderful story, untold until now.

Over the years, there have been two urgent phone calls from Commissioner Pete Rozelle to our home in the late evening hours. The first was to tell me on a Thursday evening in 1965 that the NFL was going to move into Atlanta that Saturday, "to head off the AFL," as he so frankly put it. In the same breath, in that frank description of NFL versus AFL, Pete added, "Keep your pants on, no need to run to the AFL; New Orleans will be next. You've proven yourselves with those preseason games and attendance at all of our league meetings. Atlanta will be our fifteenth city and New Orleans will be our sixteenth the following year. A perfect regional rival for Atlanta."

I believed him. I regarded Pete Rozelle as an honorable man who spoke for the owners. I also knew that a football league needs an even number of franchises for scheduling reasons. Otherwise, every week during the season, one team would be idle.

So, New Orleans was "in," or so it seemed. The battle had been won roughly six long years after that telephone call to Chep Morrison in 1960. Alleluia! Sure enough, we did become the sixteenth franchise, right on schedule for the 1967 season, arriving on All Saints Day, November 1, 1966, at a big announcement at the Pontchartrain Hotel. But it wasn't as simple as it had promised to be when Pete Rozelle told me, "New Orleans will be next." Tumultuous months lay ahead. In fact, over the many years nothing in our efforts to get New Orleans into the NFL and to get the Superdome built came easily, except the unflinching support of John McKeithen, our champion, and the great Hale Boggs.

When the NFL moved into Atlanta, the AFL, denied that city and knowing that New Orleans was committed to the NFL, had moved into Miami, becoming a nine-city league. During the following months it became apparent to both leagues that they were bleeding what promised to be endless financial blood, that the ultimate solution to their battles over players and cities was peace, peace in the form of a merger. I was aware of this development. The difficulty for the two leagues was the fact that a merger almost certainly would be perceived as a violation of anti-trust laws. What they desperately needed was a Congressional exemption from such laws, limited only to their merger.

Such a merger also would change the arithmetic for both leagues. Nine AFL franchises plus fifteen NFL franchises would be twenty-four, an even number, which would make scheduling problems for both leagues disappear. However, it also would mean that New Orleans would be out in the cold, regardless of informal franchise commitments. Even though Pete Rozelle had told me that New Orleans would be next, that number, twenty-four, still sent a chill up and down my spine.

The second nighttime telephone call from Pete Rozelle to our home came rather late one evening, near midnight in New York. Pete stated the obvious right off the bat. Their anti-trust exemption bill, the merger, was hung up in the House Judiciary Committee, dominated by its chairman, one Emanuel Celler, a Democrat from Brooklyn quite capable of keeping that merger bill tied up in his committee forever. Mr. Celler was a tough, crusty, wonderful old gentleman, who had decided that the merger would be bad for the players and millions of football fans. He probably was correct, but I can understand a counter-view that a merger would be good for the players' job stability and for fans, rescuing a number of unprofitable, perhaps failing franchise locations. I also knew that New Orleans' admission to the NFL would be ensured if somehow we could help the NFL and the AFL make that merger a reality.

During that nighttime telephone call Pete Rozelle described their problems with Mr. Celler, then asked whether I knew Congressman Joe Waggonner, a member of Mr. Celler's committee, a good man, a Democrat from the Shreveport area. Might Mr. Waggonner persuade Mr. Celler to be less obstinate?

Frankly, I was amazed that Pete thought Joe Waggonner might be of help. As gently as possible, I said that a guy like Emanuel Celler was not going to be dissuaded by a Joe Waggonner, no matter how effective he might be—or by anyone else, except possibly a well-directed political power play. I then asked the commissioner whether he knew Hale Boggs, who just might be sufficiently influential and persuasive as House majority whip to seek such a huge favor from Congressman Celler.

Pete asked, "Oh, you know Hale Boggs?" Pete's question surprised me, but I replied, "Yes, I do, but our chief racial-political adviser [this was the racially unsettled mid-1960s], David Kleck, also advises Mr. Boggs, and I can put him on a plane to Washington tomorrow morning." Pete said, "That would be wonderful," and he thanked me effusively for volunteering Mr. Kleck's services.

I added, "You know, Pete, Hale used to be a 90.1 percent winner in elections, but in 1965 he was one of the few Southern members of Congress who had the guts to support the Voting Rights Act, and now he is a 54.1 percent election winner. He needs our help as much as we need his, so perhaps Hale can restore his voter popularity if he helps New Orleans get into the NFL." With that, our conversation ended.

I put David Kleck on the plane to Washington the next morning. Kleck was a great Boggs admirer, as was I, and he agreed that Hale's political popularity could benefit enormously from any participation he might have in helping to obtain the long-sought-after franchise. I cautioned David sternly and emphatically about the significance of the number twenty-four and asked him to emphasize that point to Hale. NFL owners understandably are almost always against expansion, which to them is dilution, as I had learned the hard way. Consequently, rescue of the NFL-AFL merger bill must be tied to an absolute commitment of an immediate expansion franchise for New Orleans. Anything less would be harmful to our cause, I repeated several times. And, then, several more times.

David Kleck carried out my explicit instructions exactly as we discussed when I put him on that plane to Washington. Sure enough, our House majority whip, who knew the rules of Congress as well as anyone, conferred with his friend and ally, Russell Long, chairman of the Senate Finance Committee, who quietly attached the NFL-AFL Antitrust Exemption Bill to a Foreign Aid Tax Bill, of all things. Now came the real battle. In the House, where non-germane attachments to bills were prohibited by rule, Hale went all-out over several days to persuade super-powerful House speaker Wilbur Mills to make this one exception. Finally, Speaker Mills yielded. Hale had prevailed magnificently.

Though some believe Long alone was responsible for engineering the final steps in achieving our city's franchise, it was a Hale Boggs-Russell Long joint venture. Hale executed the one difficult, seemingly impossible step of persuading Speaker Wilbur Mills to lift the stalled NFL-AFL merger bill from Emanuel Celler's House Judiciary Committee, still attached to that Foreign Aid Tax Bill (a brilliant Long stratagem, because as a pet project of Pres. Lyndon Johnson, it was virtually assured of passage) where it would be greeted in conference by the Senate Finance Committee chairman, who just happened to be Russell Long. These were masterful politicians.

With that merger, the people of our city made near-billionaires out of all NFL owners, including in later years our own Tom Benson. Current commissioner Roger Goodell knows that the NFL owes New Orleans, big time. The merger and that crucial, critical assistance from Hale Boggs and Russell Long made the NFL what it is today, a huge, extremely successful enterprise. The commissioner recognizes that NFL obligation and is acting accordingly. The New Orleans Saints are not going anywhere.

At the time of the merger I thought Pete Rozelle naïvely believed a Congressional committee member could persuade a chairman as powerful as Emanuel Celler to change his position on such an important matter. In fact, it was I who was naïve. I was "used" but willingly and pleasantly so—and honorably. Though years later I read or heard somewhere that there is a very thin line of legality in offering something to a member of Congress in return for his or her vote, I remember nothing done by me or by the commissioner that could have been questioned legally. I have become convinced that Pete Rozelle was advised by league attorneys in advance of his telephone call to me, which, of course, was a correct action, and that Pete knew my association with Hale Boggs. By that time he probably knew that my racial-political adviser, David Kleck, also was an adviser to Hale Boggs. And Pete most certainly would know that I would be very willing to help. He also must have known of Hale's political peril created by his courageous vote of conscience in favor of the Voting Rights Act. Besides, I doubt that I was placed in legal peril; what I wanted was of a positive civic nature. I've never even asked for help with Super Bowl tickets, from what I can remember.

Fortunately, Hale Boggs built up his 54.1 percent voter approval to something in the upper 60s and was never again in political danger. I admired Hale tremendously, a masterful parliamentarian. His actions cemented the deal we had worked years to achieve.

We were getting close, very close, but as the official vote in Congress loomed, instinct told me that I should send David Kleck back to Washington, which I did, instructing him again that fifteen plus nine equals twenty-four, an even number, and no problem with scheduling. The next day Kleck was walking the Rotunda with Hale and Pete Rozelle roughly one hour before the formal vote would take place. He reported this conversation between Hale and Pete:

"Hale, the NFL is very, very appreciative of what you are doing. I just can't thank you enough."

Hale instantly questioned, "What do you mean, you can't thank me enough? New Orleans gets an immediate franchise in the NFL. Isn't that our deal?"

The commissioner replied, "I'm going to do everything I can to bring it about." Pete's reply was certainly no franchise commitment. Very disappointing, but predictable.

With that Hale turned abruptly, seemingly rushing back to his office, mumbling, "The vote is off!" According to Kleck, Pete caught up to Hale with two giant strides, turned him around gently, and said, "It's a deal, you can count on it!"

Again, according to my eyewitness, Hale Boggs, something of a patrician who rarely used strong language, said, "It better be, or you will regret it the rest of your blanking life," using the worst of the "blankings."

Why hadn't the masterful Hale Boggs officially tied everything down in advance of the important vote? My belief is that Hale intentionally refrained from securing the official commitment for a New Orleans franchise until the absolutely last moment, just one-half hour before a final vote in Congress. At that instant Pete Rozelle could not confer with his lawyer, nor could he telephone key owners, whose loose lips could have created problems for all. Hale knew that Rozelle could not let that merger get away, and in order to ensure that the bill would pass, he had to commit himself unequivocally, which he did. The NFL's brilliant commissioner in that great moment of truth had just been "had" by one of history's truly gifted political strategists, the great Thomas Hale Boggs. Though Russell Long played his role in the Senate, on vote day, the final scene belonged to Hale, who so deftly and quickly picked Pete Rozelle's franchise pocket and — *bingo!* — emerged with the New Orleans Saints.

That is how our hard-won franchise arrived. Now we were just around the corner from full, public acknowledgement of a major league football team.

November 1, 1966

Pete Rozelle called me in mid-November 1966, stating that, at last, New Orleans really was next, that at his recommendation NFL owners had settled on New Orleans as the sixteenth franchise of the National Football League.

"What do you think about an announcement day of November 1?" he asked. I laughed and said, "So you like my name, Saints?" I loved Pete's reply: "It's a perfect name for a New Orleans team, with that song and everything." So, why not officially introduce the team on All Saints Day? How fitting that our New Orleans Saints became a reality on All Saints Day in a city that had always observed the day as a religious holiday. Few schools were open; many businesses and City Hall were closed. Pete later claimed that All Saints Day was just a "coincidence."

Immediately, I told Pete that I wanted this to be a Hale Boggs day. He had stepped up when we asked for help. I said, "Hale Boggs and Russell Long were wonderful, and there are a few nuts down here who would like to unseat them. This positive press and Boggs' and Long's prominent role in the day should get rid of those guys for good." I also emphasized, "I really want to sit in the last row, and that is where I shall sit."

One amusing result of that self-relegation was public sympathy for me and Mary, that we had been "ushered" to that last row at the Pontchartrain Hotel meeting room. Not so, absolutely not so! We "ushered" ourselves.

At long last, on November 1, 1966, our six-year effort paid off. Welcome to the major leagues New Orleans! The Saints had become a reality. Commissioner Pete Rozelle of the NFL came to New Orleans and before a standing-room-only crowd at the

November 1, 1966. "N.O. Goes Pro!" Victor Schiro and Dave Dixon admiring the *New Orleans States* announcement.

Pontchartrain Hotel pronounced our wonderful city a National Football League member. Assigned to the National Conference, we resided among the previous fifteen member NFL teams. At that point the AFL with its nine member teams became the American Conference. Cleveland, Pittsburgh, and Baltimore (later Indianapolis) agreed to become members of the American Conference, switching from the National Conference. The AFC expanded into Cincinnati. Thus the NFL was comprised of two thirteen-city conferences, later to grow through expansion to two sixteen-team conferences.

Today, most of the events of that day are a blur. I wanted the attention to be focused on Hale Boggs so that his position in Congress as a future Speaker of the House could be strengthened. As I had explained to commissioner Rozelle, Hale's status with the electorate had been weakened considerably, even perilously, by the shrill voices and influence of every racist and radical-right voter in his district after he voted for the Voting Rights Act of 1965. Hale had performed skillfully as a legislator when he rescued the NFL-AFL merger bill in the House, combining with Russell Long in the Senate to ensure passage of that legislation, the final peg in the final hole for our city's NFL franchise, so I wanted this day to be about those two political geniuses . . . and it was. Hale was never again in political peril.

Mary Dixon whispered to me as the press flash bulbs were popping, "If all those clowns standing up at the front getting their pictures taken and taking credit for getting the franchise had helped us from the beginning, we would have had the New Orleans Saints here three years ago." Maybe so, maybe not. I'll say one thing, though: that girl Mary is almost always right.

Help from a Higher Power

People ask where and how we came up with the names "Saints" and "Superdome." "Saints" was a cinch because of the internationally famous and favorite local song "When the Saints Go Marching In." However, Archbishop Philip M. Hannan also played a role in settling on the name, eliminating forever any question of what our team should be called.

Archbishop Hannan had arrived in New Orleans almost coincidentally with the team's newly appointed owner, John Mecom, Jr. Mecom had sent his Houston public relations guy, an impressive person whose name eludes me, to New Orleans to talk to me about their concern that the name "Saints" might somehow be considered sacrilegious. This was a legitimate concern but one I had already considered and discussed with various religious authorities.

We were discussing this matter over dinner at a local restaurant when I looked up and saw Archbishop Hannan walking past our table. I threw out my left arm to block his progress but stood up immediately and apologized for my unintentional rudeness. I then related to the archbishop our discussion regarding the naming of the team.

He said immediately, "Oh, I think 'Saints' is a wonderful name for our team. Nothing sacrilegious at all." He paused, and then added, "Besides, I have this terrible premonition that we might need all the help we can get."

That settled the name issue. But I've always felt that his premonition might have inspired the famous prayer that our beloved archbishop delivered before the very first regular season game of our Saints in September 1967, a prayer so memorable that many in attendance at the 83,000-person sellout still recall the moment:

Prayer for Our Saints

God, we ask your blessing upon all who participate in this event, and all who have supported our Saints. Our heavenly father who has instructed us that the "saints by faith conquered kingdoms . . . and overcame lions," grant our Saints an increase of faith and strength so that they will not only overcome the Lions, but also the Bears, the Rams, the Giants, and even those awesome people in Green Bay.

May they continue to tame the Redskins and fetter the Falcons as well as the Eagles. Give to our owners and coaches the continued ability to be as wise as serpents and as simple as doves, so that no good talent will dodge our draft. Grant to our fans perseverance in their devotion and unlimited lung power, tempered with a sense of charity to all, including the referees.

May our beloved "Bedlam Bowl" [Tulane Stadium] be a source of good fellowship and may the "Saints Come Marching In" be a victory march for all, now and in eternity.

Philip M. Hannan
Archbishop of New Orleans

As for "Superdome," that one was easy. I selected the name early on, right at the beginning of our stadium and franchise efforts. Actually, I chose the name while the Astrodome was still a mammoth hole in the ground over in Houston. I considered only two names, Superdome or Ultradome. To my ear "Superdome" sounded far better than "Ultradome." So it was Louisiana Superdome when I first visited Gov. John McKeithen about building a stadium, years before there was a Super Bowl. The Superdome's initial board of commissioners ultimately confirmed the Louisiana Superdome.

A Majority Owner

Just over a month after the Saints dream became a reality, the team had its first majority owner, John Mecom, Jr., of Houston, Texas. I must admit that not a day goes by, even today, that I do not figuratively kick myself for failing to take full advantage of the Lamar Hunt opportunity back in 1962-63. The regret is especially strong when I think of Mecom and the nineteen years of

John Mecom, Pete Rozell, and Dave Dixon, December 18, 1967. (© 2007 The Times-Picayune Publishing Co. All rights reserved. Used with permission of The Times-Picayune.)

sad performance under him, with not even one winning season, not even a .500 season. Mr. Mecom, and any minority ownership participants with whom he might have been associated, were not very successful, particularly if we were to grade on the basis of a win-loss record, which was the worst in the NFL for their ownership period. Seven head coaches, I believe. Pretty bad; in fact, terrible. And then Tom Benson, perhaps the least publicly friendly owner in the NFL, is a mystery person to this day.

The problem began with Commissioner Pete Rozelle's requirement that one individual be majority owner. Each franchise, Rozelle said, must have one voice and one voice only. Such a policy prevented in-house squabbles at league meetings. Though it was probably a sound stipulation, its benefits were limited by the fact that individual egos have open season in the NFL.

My associates and I (Edward B. Poitevent, Sonny Westfeldt, Robert Monsted, Hugh M. Evans, and William G. Helis, Jr.) could not find a person locally who was qualified to be majority owner. Through Edward Poitevent, a senior partner in the law firm Jones, Walker, Waechter, Poitevent, Carrere and Denegre, we hit upon a solid prospect. Edward's firm handled the considerable legal requirements and Louisiana activities of the great oil producer John Mecom, well regarded, based in nearby Houston, and worth hundreds of millions of 1966 dollars and easily capable of handling the $9 million expansion franchise fee. John Mecom, Sr., would put ownership in the hands of his son, John Mecom, Jr. All of this was very attractive, so after meeting John, Jr., his wife, and his parents, we agreed to give the Mecoms our support. Frankly, at that point we had no real choice.

Everything seemed to be going well, but I soon began to have nagging doubts about John, Jr.'s, sense of responsibility. He rarely returned telephone calls, and when he did, it always took a long time. This was irritating and not very bright, because I had a strong enough position with NFL owners that if I, a New Orleans native and the individual who had done all the work for years, were to object to John, Jr., of Houston, Texas, then the

NFL owners would respond accordingly, especially if there were a suitable alternative. Eventually, I decided that this mostly likable, attractive young guy would be more responsive if he set up shop in our city. Later I realized that this was an unfortunate decision.

I was still in John, Jr.'s corner, though, when the NFL Expansion Committee came to New Orleans for a final check of the three major applicants: John Mecom, Jr.; a second group headed by Herman Lay of Frito-Lay and Edgar B. Stern, Jr., of New Orleans (an outstanding person who was extremely well connected and highly regarded in New Orleans); and a third individual applicant, Louis J. Roussel, a powerful, wealthy, colorful, and controversial New Orleans oil man, whom I knew fairly well through mutual family friends, particularly the family of Dr. Francis LeJeune of New Orleans, of whom I was enormously fond.

At that time I expected the committee to rubber-stamp approval of John, Jr. The committee was composed of three NFL powerhouses: Mr. George Halas, the most influential of all league owners, still the very active founder and patriarch of the NFL; Lamar Hunt, a close friend and founder of the AFL; and Carroll Rosenbloom, owner of the famous Baltimore Colts. All three came straight to the point, making a lead statement delivered by Carroll Rosenbloom that astounded me, followed by a very direct question, along these lines: "Dave, all three of us agree that without you there would be no New Orleans franchise, so whomever you select who is qualified almost certainly will be the person or group that the three of us will recommend. Now, are you sure you are still okay with John Mecom, Jr.?" I was stunned, gave the comment some split-second thinking, and decided that I should not hesitate. After just the tiniest pause, I said, "Yes, John is okay by me."

They asked me that question in sort of a reception atmosphere, with dozens of people milling around. If the conversation had been in a private room, as it should have been, I probably would have expressed my uncertainty, telling them that he seemed a bit indecisive and not very knowledgeable. He didn't return phone calls; perhaps he was a little bit young and immature.

I might also have added, though I did not, that I had heard a solidly based rumor that Bedford Wynne, who owned about 10 percent of the Cowboys, was going to sell or give to Tex Schramm his share so that Schramm might have an ownership stake in the Cowboys. Supposedly, Bedford was going to be given free of charge a like percentage of the Saints for Tex Schramm's and Clint Murchison's "help" in getting the franchise for Mecom. This latter bit of information had stunned me. What role did Schramm or the Cowboys play, other than the fact that Pete Rozelle and Tex Schramm were close friends from their L.A. Rams days? Edward Poitevent's law firm had uncovered Mecom months earlier. And I personally had "sold" New Orleans to every NFL and AFL owner and to Pete Rozelle. Widespread reaction by individual NFL owners to this arrangement would have been unpredictable.

Had I been required to make a decision on the spot in a private-room conversation, I probably would have said that my preference was for Edgar Stern, Jr., whom I liked and admired, and Herman Lay. I had nothing against Bedford Wynne and certainly not against Tex Schramm. I simply thought it was wrong and improper for Tex to acquire stock in the Cowboys at New Orleans' expense, if indeed the facts as I learned them were correct. Lay and Stern, Jr., would have been excellent owners, and our city would have been spared the many unhappy hours of the Mecom era. Moreover, we would not have lost one of our finest citizens, Edgar Stern, Jr., now living in the Pacific Northwest.

However, I was torn by a similar regard for Louis Roussel, who lived and worked in New Orleans. A true New Orleanian and a very, very tough businessman, Roussel, a former streetcar conductor, was not particularly acceptable to "upper crust" New Orleans or the local power structure, nor to Tulane University where the Saints would play for eight seasons. However, I knew him pretty well, and I thought he would learn the football business perhaps quicker than anyone in the world. I believe he would have won at least two or three Super Bowls . . . or killed someone or himself trying. There would have been no discussion of Mr. Roussel moving the franchise out of New Orleans, ever. He was a New Orleanian. Nevertheless, I would have recommended Edgar Stern, Jr., and Herman Lay as Saints owners.

Instead I went with the Mecoms, tentatively accepting their offer to be chairman of the board of the New Orleans Saints primarily because I realized that the Mecoms had the votes. Sure enough, I soon saw Bedford Wynne in New Orleans, always around Mecom, apparently running things, making a trade of the number-one pick in the draft, the great Bubba Smith, to the Baltimore Colts for a nice young quarterback named Gary Cuozzo, who was promptly beaten out of his job with the Saints by Billy Kilmer, an expansion-pool player. It was Bedford Wynne, I believe, who made the deal with the Colts. A second-string quarterback for the number-one pick in the draft. Bedford, a good guy, was not the football man that he thought. (Incidentally, Billy Kilmer was one of the two or three great football competitors of all time in my book, and a super guy).

Within just a couple of weeks I realized that I had made a mistake recommending what turned out to be a Bedford Wynne-John Mecom, Jr., entourage and said so privately to Gov. John McKeithen, with whom I had become friends while pursing an NFL team for the city. As chairman of the board of the Louisiana Stadium and Exposition District, he promptly told me that he had never accepted my resignation as executive director of the Superdome commission, which I had submitted to become chairman of the board of the Saints, and he wanted me to return to my position immediately. "Welcome back," he said. There was a happy ending. Working for and with John McKeithen was a pleasure, a truly great adventure.

As for John Mecom, Jr., my dealings with him were always pleasant. He was a likable young guy thrust into a position that twenty years later he might have handled very well indeed. I am sorry that things did not work out for John with the New Orleans Saints.

My unquestioned friend, Bill Connick (who once worked for Mr. Louis Roussel) told me years later that "Mister Louis" felt betrayed by U.S. senator Russell Long, who supposedly was going to "obtain" the franchise for him. One thing I know for sure, Russell Long was in no position to deliver the Saints franchise to anyone. "Mr. Louis" had been misled, for what reason I still have no explanation.

The other thing I recognize is that had I known for certain that the rumor was true, that Tex Schramm was to acquire Bedford Wynne's Cowboys stock in some form or other while Bedford acquired Saints stock, I would have answered Carroll Rosenbloom's question with these words: "My choice is either Lay and Stern or Mr. Louis Roussel." Upon close questioning I would have stated the Schramm-Wynne relationship as my reason. This, unfortunately, might have caused grief for Pete Rozelle, assuming his knowledge of what was happening. Pete was a good friend whom I liked and respected.

Those things said, and off my mind and my conscience, let's turn to the exhilarating first Saints game.

New Orleans Saints vs. the Los Angeles Rams

Almost six and a half years after the day that New Orleans mayor de Lesseps "Chep" Morrison, one of the three great New Orleans mayors of my lifetime, asked me to be chairman of his Major League Sports Committee, we had won the battle. The "we" being my family and I plus a tight little group of believers, four personal friends, all prominent New Orleans business and civic leaders, Edward Poitevent, Robert Monsted, George Westfeldt, and Hugh Evans.

There they were, our New Orleans Saints, a brand-new expansion team, the sixteenth member of the National Football League, about to receive the opening kickoff from the mighty Los Angeles Rams coached by the legendary George Allen, right here in New Orleans, Louisiana, in wonderful old Tulane Stadium. It was September 17, 1967, and the first kickoff was in the air. Waiting at the goal line was the Saints rookie running back-wide receiver, a superb, fine-looking physical specimen, a late first-round pick with blazing speed, one John Gilliam, for whom the Saints and their head coach, Tom Fears (a great old Rams wide receiver) had high hopes.

All 81,209 of us had been witnesses to the finest pre-game prayer ever delivered by anyone, anywhere, anytime by our incredibly popular Archbishop Philip M. Hannan. The stage was set: great prayers, sellout crowd, new team, perfect day.

Indeed, as we waited for that first kickoff, a fleeting, almost ghostlike thought went through my mind. I thought back to a few of the great Tulane running backs of Green Wave glory days, before 1949's sad de-emphasis: "Brother" Brown, Bill Banker, Don Zimmerman, "Little Monk" Simons, "Bronco" Brunner, Bucky Bryan, Preacher Roberts, Jitterbug Kellogg, Eddie Price, almost all of whom had run back big kickoffs at this great old facility. But none of those plays were as big or more timely than the one we were about to see.

John Gilliam caught that opening kickoff near the goal line and took off! He juked a couple of Rams at the 18, brushed off another tackler at the 22, and by the time he hit his own 30 he suddenly appeared to be "gone." He was indeed "gone," and all 81,209 Saints fans seemed to know it at the same moment. Hell, I think my Mary Dixon knew he was "gone" at that 18 yard line "juke," because at that insane moment she jumped to her feet, proclaiming, "He's gone!" The loudest touchdown roar, per-haps in American football history—certainly in New Orleans history—erupted. A close friend of ours swore to me that he heard that Tulane Stadium "roar" as he left his downtown office building. A brief moment after John Gilliam danced into the end zone, my beautiful Mary Dixon put her arms around me, and said, "Well, sweetheart, we did it." I confess that tears came to my eyes, but if those circumstances wouldn't make you choke up, what would? What a moment for great old Tulane Stadium! I was beside myself with joy for our Saints.

When they tore down Tulane Stadium years later, I cut up a few of the seats. I still have the two seats Mary and I occupied during John Gilliam's monumental, unforgettable kickoff return: section GG, row 24, seats 15 and 16.

As John Gilliam returned the opening kickoff for a fantastic touchdown, I noticed that my friend Buddy Diliberto, covering the game for the *Picayune*, picked up Gilliam at the Saints 30 and raced with him all the way along the sideline to the Saints 35 (5 yards total), accompanied by my friend, Ro Brown of Channel 6. Actually, Ro made it to the end zone, Diliberto fainted at the 35. Delirium, pure delirium!

The Saints lost 27 to 13, but it was superb NFL entertainment. The Saints were in New Orleans, and they were ours!

CHAPTER VI

The Superdome Campaign

During the years I worked to convince the NFL to grant New Orleans a franchise, I was simultaneously seeking to secure for the team a place to play. My first semiserious thoughts about a new stadium had begun in 1964, two years before New Orleans went pro. Tulane University had been very gracious, but I could see that a new stadium, probably a domed one, was the ultimate answer for our city. I actually designed a rectangular stadium model with a sliding roof, made of corrugated fiberboard. A sliding roof! A bit ahead of my time. A very talented young man, Peter Briant, brother of an equally talented close friend and good neighbor Andrée Lago, helped me with this little project, my first Superdome model.

I knew that the residential area surrounding Tulane Stadium was not well suited for half a dozen crowds of 70,000 or better each fall. I sensed, too, that Tulane desperately needed room for campus expansion, and a new stadium where Tulane could play its own games would be greeted with much enthusiasm by Pres. Herbert Longenecker and Tulane's Board of Administrators. Tulane encouraged me and was very cooperative and helpful.

It seemed safe to say that five of the six groups of support we originally had hoped to solidify when bringing in an NFL team were strongly in our corner. It was obvious that we had the full support of the people of New Orleans. Indeed, we had a survey taken during the middle 1960s by a top national TV consultant, Frank Magid & Associates (who did extensive research analysis work for Channel 4, WWL-TV). The survey showed that 94 percent of the people in the area supported our efforts to bring New Orleans into the National Football League. The Sugar Bowl executives, Tulane, the fans, the TV and radio people, and area black leadership were solidly with us, but The Editor would remain a problem for several more years. I finally learned to avoid that individual and concentrate on TV and radio.

This incredibly favorable report and solid community support, all of which I learned later had made a strong impression on our incoming governor, John J. McKeithen, probably was due to our focus on obtaining the support of everyone associated with local TV and radio — WDSU-TV (NBC), WWL-TV (CBS), WWL radio, ABC, WSMB, WNOE, WTIX — to make up for the lack of support at the *Times-Picayune,* though my wonderful friend Buddy Diliberto would sneak in an occasional, always supportive column, probably when The Editor was out of town.

Our hard work at courting TV and radio affiliates had paid off. Supporters included the late A. Louis Read, president of WDSU-TV when they ranked first in the market, as well as Mel Leavitt, Alec Gifford, and Jerry Romig. At WWL, we found support from Mike Early and the wonderful Jesuits with always positive Angela Hill as an anchor and rock-solid Hap Glaudi as sports anchor, later the great Jim Henderson (many rate Jim as the best sports anchor in America) and such stalwarts as Ed Daniels at ABC26 (WGNO). I do not remember anything but whole-hearted support from local TV and radio.

The old *New Orleans States-Item* (an afternoon paper) was also a positive force with Carl Corbin, Harry Martinez, Peter Finney, and the great Walter Cowan, who conducted a pivotal interview with the Committee of Deans of Engineering, Environmental Design, and Architecture at LSU and Tulane, Roger Richardson, Gerald McLendon, and John Lawrence respectively. Their presence led to the critical victory of the stadium commission's recommending and endorsing the selection of Superdome architects and engineers based strictly on merit.

The Vic Schiro Fireside Chat

In late 1964, a great battle for the mayor's office was brewing in New Orleans that, incredibly, would have a positive impact on both of our major efforts, franchise and Superdome. The incumbent, Victor Hugo Schiro, a dapper, likable, but at times unintentionally amusing figure ("If it's good for New Orleans, I'm for it."), was facing a strong challenge from the popular, very bright, well-liked councilman at large, Jimmy Fitzmorris. The race figured to be a tossup.

(Another famous Schiroism uttered by our mayor, dressed in Castro cap and fatigues, during the frightening Hurricane Betsy is the unforgettable "Don't believe any false rumors unless they come from your mayor." Today I believe that our clever mayor's redundancy with "false rumors" was intentional.)

We had been looking for land for a possible new stadium. I had secured a commitment of sorts from the principal Avon heir, David McConnell, an enormously wealthy and likable New Yorker and a Medal of Honor winner from Guadalcanal, who promised to put up 100 percent of the figure being bounced around as an NFL expansion franchise fee if the city would provide the land for a new stadium.

We also approached Edgar B. Stern, Jr., who would have been a wonderful 100 percent owner: "Not interested." In hindsight I should have worked on Lester Kabacoff, his chief assistant and an extremely bright civic ball of fire who might very well have converted Edgar, a really nice person, a great citizen, but not a football fan. Edgar eventually left New Orleans, a huge civic loss. He would have been loved as owner of our New Orleans Saints, because he would have been a great owner.

A New York area land developer named Marvin Kratter had gained control, by all reports, of thousands of acres in the New Orleans East area. He had offered 155 acres, well located, to Mayor Schiro free of charge for a new stadium for an NFL franchise that many New Orleanians now felt was inevitable.

Our public relations coordinator and political consultant, David Kleck, had been informed by Mr. Kratter's people and by the Schiro forces that the 155-acre site was available free for any NFL expansion owner, provided I would appear on TV with Mayor Schiro with our stadium model and explain the novel ideas we had for such a facility. In effect, they were asking me to endorse Mayor Schiro.

At that point I had never been involved in politics. I liked Victor Schiro, but I leaned toward his opponent, Jimmy Fitzmorris, a very popular councilman at large. Mr. Kleck told me that the Schiro people and Marvin Kratter thought the mayor would be re-elected and that most likely my appearance and semi-endorsement would not be necessary. Further, Mr. Kratter said that the 155 acres would be available even if I did not appear, unless requested, and even if Fitzmorris won. But I was required to appear on TV and to support Mayor Schiro if requested to do so in order to clinch the free land deal.

I felt, after long agonizing, "Who am I to turn down millions of dollars of land for our city?" I had visited the proposed area. It was high and dry after a major storm, an excellent stadium site, even if not quite perfect. Besides, our Avon heir and potential NFL owner, David McConnell, had visited the site with his group, which included one William Wallace, my good friend from NFL meetings and chief NFL reporter for the *New York Times.* So I agreed, crossing my fingers that I would never have to appear on TV to endorse Schiro.

Off to New York I went to court Pete Rozelle and other NFL executives, to see Bill Wallace and David McConnell, and to "politick" the media and advertisers on behalf of our city. I quietly politicked the AFL people a bit, visiting AFL commissioner Joe Foss and my old friend Lamar Hunt, just in case it ever became necessary to jump the NFL ship.

By then I guess I was becoming more and more political in relation to the football leagues and probably had reached a point where I could "preach it either way," NFL or AFL. Buddy Diliberto wrote a column stating that on the wall facing the entrance to my office in the Hibernia Bank Building hung either a picture of Pete Rozelle with a shelf underneath holding an autographed NFL ball or a picture of Joe Foss, with an autographed AFL ball on the shelf, depending on who might be visiting. Not quite true, but I did have the pictures and the footballs. I remember that Lamar Hunt, then AFL, commented favorably. Rozelle was hilariously amused.

Still in New York, I relaxed a bit as we neared the Saturday election. It was the Wednesday prior and there had been no

Dave Dixon, Victor and Sunny Schiro, and Hale Boggs, viewing Superdome model.

request for my presence at a televised "fireside chat." Mayor Schiro had undergone an emergency appendectomy and was convalescing at home, supposedly ahead in the polls. However, when the phone rang in my hotel room at 6 P.M., I feared the worst. Sure enough, it was David Kleck, stating that the mayoralty polls were now very, very close. Further, I would have to participate in the fireside chat from Mayor Schiro's home on Thursday evening, the very next day. Marvin Kratter would be there to make the pledge to the mayor and to me, and I was to bring the impressive stadium model we had developed. I had to rush to the airport to catch the last flight that evening from New York, accomplished with only moments to spare.

True to his word Marvin Kratter repeated his 155-acre land pledge to me privately before the show and then publicly. Mayor Schiro looked very dapper in his gentleman's robe and appeared happy and excited over the donation of the free land, which all of us thought was a giant step toward an NFL franchise. My stadium model was impressive and effective, and I didn't stammer too much in implied admiration and approval of Mayor Schiro's statements. The televised chat probably was a political masterstroke by the mayor's forces.

The next morning, Friday, the *Times-Picayune*'s front-page story was very strong in its support of Schiro and the Superdome. Poor Jimmy Fitzmorris, all he could do was agree that whatever happened regarding a stadium, it should be good for the city.

The next day was election day. To my great surprise it was a "squeaker." Mayor Schiro won reelection by less than 800 votes. According to David Kleck, the fireside chat had been worth at least 5,000 votes. John McKeithen later claimed it had garnered Schiro "at least 8,000 votes, no question about it." Jimmy Fitzmorris, a distinguished public servant, likely lost the post that had been his lifelong goal as a result of this fireside chat. I apologized to Jimmy for my participation, which he accepted with grace, saying, "David, you were my friend before all of this, and you will always be my friend."

The Gubernatorial Force Behind the Superdome

Our Louisiana Superdome sits in all its splendor on Poydras Street because, primarily, we had an always honorable Louisiana governor, John McKeithen. With careful analysis and heavy thought in later years, from the vantage point of many hundreds of hours together, countless visits to the governor's mansion in Baton Rouge, trips to New York and Washington with him, and calls upon him at his home in Columbia, knowing him so well that I was even aware of the few minor deficiencies every person possesses, I have reached the following summarization of John McKeithen: He was a person of great intelligence, integrity, imagination, and courage who possessed a surprisingly clear vision of the future. McKeithen was a political giant in many respects who, I honestly believe, would have been president of the United States if he had been governor of Illinois, Ohio,

"Louisiana will have the finest Stadium in the entire world!"
A Message From Governor John J. McKeithen

"The domed stadium is an investment that will benefit the state by over $150 million in the first year and will mark the beginning of an era of increased national prestige for Louisiana."

"Approval of the constitutional amendment making the dome stadium a reality was the greatest thing that's happened to the State since the Louisiana Purchase."

"Having seen the Astrodome in Houston makes me all the more certain we're right in building such a facility in New Orleans, which has sports tradition, population and economic growth, and which can outdraw Houston any day."

"So, how can we afford not to build a showplace which will be enjoyed by our children, grandchildren and great grandchildren?"

"The domed stadium will be two generations beyond anything in existence in the world today."

John McKeithen's support of the Superdome.

Pennsylvania, New York, or California. As it was, he nearly became president from Louisiana, a fascinating story to be told in depth later herein, never to my knowledge told anywhere before and known only to perhaps four persons living today.

But in 1964, I knew none of this. That year, I had invited as a matter of course newly elected governor John McKeithen to a small pre-game reception at the New Orleans Country Club for visiting officials from Green Bay and St. Louis. I was shocked when he actually appeared, unannounced, and even more surprised when he whispered in my ear that he was an *"enormous"* football fan and promised to help us in any way possible. In fact, at first I did not even recognize our new governor. Frankly, I didn't take his comments very seriously at the time. I'd heard the same thing from other politicians. Months later, when I came to know our new governor well, I realized that John McKeithen was every bit as much a football fan as I.

The American people are obsessed with this great spectator sport at high school, college, and professional levels. We have used the power of football to great advantage in recent years in Sugar Bowls and Super Bowls and with the Saints and the Superdome. Unfortunately, my alma mater, Tulane, to this day misunderstands and underrates the political power of football. John McKeithen said to me on several occasions, quite pointedly, "To know that football is king in the U.S. is a basic political wisdom!"

So it was with McKeithen's earnest passion for football in mind that I approached him for help with the Superdome. By early 1965, I had become convinced that our Avon heir, David McConnell, was perhaps a bit disinterested and not dedicated enough to be a good owner. Besides, I had increasingly private doubts about the land deal in New Orleans East as a Superdome site. I had come to think Downtown, even if only vaguely. A meeting with Governor McKeithen arranged by a friend, legislator Sal Anzelmo from New Orleans, had become one of great importance, and I had prepared myself carefully. It was just the governor and I.

As the meeting began I emphasized the versatility of our Superdome compared to Houston's much-touted Astrodome, "basically a baseball stadium with a roof over it." I was already using the term "Louisiana Superdome." And the "Saints" had become part of my daily vocabulary because of the great song "When the Saints Go Marching In," played 365 days a year in New Orleans (and elsewhere frequently). I explained to Governor McKeithen that businesses would be able to use the stadium for conventions, trade shows, and meeting rooms, it would be available for basketball and baseball conversion, and it would be "the best football stadium in the world, light years ahead of Houston." It would be the beginning of a huge new hospitality convention industry for our state.

I spoke uninterruptedly for about twenty minutes. There were no questions. Governor McKeithen had put his feet on his desk. He seemed to be listening intently, but said nothing. I couldn't read him. He stirred only slightly — but significantly — when I knocked down Houston. Finally, I slowed down, and he asked, "Is that it, Mr. Dixon?" "Yes, that's it, Governor," I replied, thinking I had struck out.

Well, our governor took his feet off his desk, slowly rose, raised his fist (at that precise particle of a second I somehow knew the battle was won) and slammed it down on his desk, proclaiming, "My God, that would be the greatest building in the history of mankind! We'll build that sucker," almost simultaneously calling his secretary, Rita Vicknair, to come into his office and to ask Judge Carlos Spaht, his chief administrative officer and a much-respected figure in Louisiana politics, to join her. It was Judge Spaht who developed the concept of a Louisiana Stadium and Exposition District created by constitutional amendment.

"Mr. Dixon," the governor said, "Tell Miss Vicknair and Judge Spaht the things you just told me." So I started all over again, even including the first concept ever of giant-screen instant replay, an idea I conceived in 1963 after I missed a great play at Tiger Stadium while buying a Coke for Mary. Judge Spaht loved the giant TV screen idea, and Rita Vicknair seemed every bit as sold as Governor McKeithen, using the same superlatives. Judge Spaht, too, was highly complimentary, asking, of course, what it would cost.

I replied, "Well, it depends on location, land, seating capacity, size, etc., and a number of other factors. However, we do have the example of the Houston Astrodome to go by, and it would seem to be quite feasible."

From that moment in Baton Rouge, John McKeithen never wavered in his support of the Louisiana Superdome. We became close personal friends and confidants, visiting each other's homes on numerous occasions.

Originally, based to an extent on Astrodome costs, we had believed that construction of the Superdome would run between $35 million and $40 million. However, a period of huge

Tom Donelan, Moon Landrieu, Gov. John McKeithen, and Dave
Dixon announcing launch of Superdome construction, 1970.

inflation in the construction industry hit us prior to and during the planning and construction of the Superdome, more than 20 percent per year for three consecutive years. Only the steadfastness and inspired leadership of John McKeithen kept our great project alive during these critical, difficult years. Harold Judell was the brilliant bond attorney who structured the bonds that financed the Superdome. If there was an essential guy in the creation of the Superdome other than McKeithen, it was Harold Judell.

The first major cost-influencing factor came when we realized that a study commissioned from Gulf South Research Institute was correct in its analysis of location factors. Of course, it should be Downtown, we all agreed. So from free land in New Orleans East we encountered land procurement costs of more than $20 million. We realized, though, that we were actually saving money in related location costs such as new roads, police and fire protection, sewerage and drainage costs, land fill, and so on, already in place. Plus preventing the fury that would have resulted from huge traffic jams before and after major events with 95 percent of traffic heading in one direction, instead of coming from all directions to the downtown area, seemed worth the initial expense.

McKeithen, once he became completely immersed in our Superdome with all its versatility and convertibility, realized that although the cost of the Superdome was much more than expected, he just might be creating a huge new industry — tourism, conventions, and trade shows — for our city and state. For him these were the great beginnings of what ultimately became today's gigantic hospitality industry in New Orleans. Finally, the location would solidify and improve the central business district, an ancillary benefit worth hundreds of millions of dollars over the years. As a direct result of the Superdome's location and the economic lessons that great building taught all of us, our multibillion-dollar tourism and convention industry was on its way to becoming major league in every aspect. Vision. John McKeithen had it, big time.

I also give former mayor Moon Landrieu, a great mayor,

tremendous credit for spotting the huge potential of major conventions from the day he hired Ed McNeil, an expert procurer of conventions and trade shows, to exploit that potential.

The cost of land would not be the Superdome's only additional expense. At that time the NFL generally favored a capacity of 50,000 to 55,000, just the right size to sell out in those days. For New Orleans they recommended 55,000. Meanwhile, the Sugar Bowl executives stated emphatically that they could not survive in a 55,000-capacity stadium, even with the higher ticket prices that would result from upholstered seating, weather protection, and other comforts and amenities. John McKeithen agreed with the Sugar Bowlers. Actually, we all agreed as we studied the whole picture more carefully.

The usual array of critics began to howl as costs went up and up, from a $40 million stadium on free land, seating perhaps 50,000, to a 71,000-capacity Superdome located in Downtown New Orleans on expensive land that we would have to buy. Memory tells me that the actual construction cost was $93 million, plus roughly $20 million in land costs, for a total of approximately $113 million.

One well-placed news media critic, a person who always took great pleasure in announcing Superdome cost "overruns," The Editor, insisted on adding $50 million in interest costs on the thirty-year bonds so that the Superdome was and still is called the "$163 million Louisiana Superdome." The Editor was still hard at work "blocking progress" but shortly he would no longer be a factor, as he was soon to retire.

I once asked Ben Levy, a top administrator for Mayor Landrieu, who had succeeded me as the Superdome's executive director when I decided to return to private life in early 1972, as the Superdome was being constructed, why the stadium committee did not point out that no building or home in America is cost-identified with thirty years of future interest added. For example, if a person pays $250,000 for a home, it is considered a $250,000 home, not a $400,000 home with thirty years of mortgage-interest costs figured in. Ben Levy said, "Dave, Moon and I figured, let our critics use whatever dollar figure they want. It will give them one less thing to complain about. Regardless of what they say, this thing is going to be a huge success. You were right, Buster Curtis [the Superdome architect] is a genius, and the building will be beautiful. They'll look like chumps."

I couldn't argue with such brilliant logic and wisdom, born probably of Ben's experiences at City Hall. I, too, call it our $163 million Louisiana Superdome, an investment that has produced many billions of dollars in civic profits and benefits for our city and state. Ben and I knew that it really was a $113 million stadium. Actually quite a bargain, wasn't it?

Ben Levy and his ever-watchful mentor, Mayor Landrieu, did a tremendous job during the Superdome construction phase. Edwin Edwards, who became governor in 1972, did an excellent job of completing the work that John McKeithen had begun. He was gracious, as always, at dedication ceremonies in 1975, giving the bulk of the credit to former governor McKeithen. The Superdome opened its doors about fourteen years from the date that a small group of friends and I set out to bring the NFL to New Orleans. Its completion was roughly eleven years from the date John McKeithen told me in his office at the state capitol in Baton Rouge, "That will be the greatest building in the history of mankind. We'll build that sucker." He didn't miss his mark by much, did he?

Constitutional Changes

Before state money could be spent on building the Superdome, the project needed to be approved by the citizens of Louisiana. There were the usual number of constitutional amendments facing Louisiana voters in a statewide election set for late November 1966, but two key amendments attracted great interest. Amendment #1 was to allow Louisiana governors to succeed themselves once, meaning that John McKeithen could run for election to a second term. Amendment #10 created the Louisiana Stadium and Exposition District, a fancy name for our Superdome and its board of commissioners. McKeithen was named chairman of the board (as governor). I was a board member chosen by Victor Schiro, the mayor of New Orleans.

During the months prior to the vote, both amendments at first

Original members of the LSED Commission, 1967.

seemed certain to pass. As time went on the enmities that traditionally divided north Louisiana and south Louisiana—and
even New Orleans and the rest of the state—began to emerge,
perhaps exacerbated by the Baton Rouge media. Some north
and central Louisiana legislators and newspapers began to
criticize both amendments. The central theme against #10 was
simple and to the point, in effect saying, "If New Orleans wants
a Superdome, let them pay for it themselves." I'm always
astounded and amused by such an attitude, with the New
Orleans metro area representing 35 percent or more of the population of Louisiana. What does it take to be a Louisiana city?

The criticism of Amendment #1 concerned the natural worry
that a two-term governor would become too powerful. While
hard to believe today, even New Orleans' own newspapers, the
Times-Picayune and the *States-Item,* though generally supportive,
became somewhat lukewarm. Governor McKeithen's closest
advisors began to tell the governor that the Superdome might

become an albatross for a still popular, highly effective governor. McKeithen himself became concerned. Polls showed that both amendments were no longer certain to be approved by voters in November. He decided to begin an intensive campaign for Amendment #1 while slightly edging away from #10. I kidded him, asking if I had become a "Dave who?"

Confiding his concern to me, he suggested that I take over the campaign for Amendment #10. Frankly, I too was concerned, yet exhilarated by the challenge and confident of my ability to defend our Superdome. Immediately, I began to telephone Rotary, Lions, and Kiwanis chapters, LSU and Tulane booster clubs, quarterback clubs, newspaper editors, radio and TV stations, and church groups, seeking speaking engagements and appointments in almost every parish in the state. I ended up with twenty-seven speaking dates and a dozen or more important appointments over the state in a period of twenty-five work days. Saturdays and Sundays were reserved for my wife and our three young sons. Such a grueling schedule today would put me in the funeral parlor at the halfway mark. Including impromptu occasions, I made more than forty speeches during that period.

The November 1, 1966, date of the Saints press conference announcing the city's successful bid in getting the team was a huge political boost to our Superdome Constitutional Amendment vote, then less than a month away. The vote now was for a real, live NFL team, the New Orleans Saints. (The name was an absolute commitment to me from John Mecom, Jr., one element in my support of his candidacy as owner of the franchise).

We won endorsements from every major newspaper in the state except the two Baton Rouge papers, which traditionally opposed many things that might be pro New Orleans, or so it seemed to some New Orleans area legislators. I found myself respecting the reasoned, conservative Superdome positions of the Manship family in Baton Rouge, owners of both newspapers and a major television station, an attitude that in hindsight might have muted their opposition just a bit. I was particularly fond of sports editor Dan Hardesty of their afternoon newspaper, the old *State-Times*. He was a good, sincere, honest man and a strong, effective critic. I became good friends with this converted Superdome critic.

My final campaign date was with the Rotary Club in Lafayette, where a packed house was waiting. I was delighted that my path crossed that of Governor McKeithen's, the first time I had seen him in thirty days. He was visiting with press, TV, and radio executives in that thriving Acadiana center. The governor asked to borrow a few minutes from my speaker's time, which of course I was happy to yield.

Wow, did he give a great speech! He was an absolute master of his trade, receiving several standing ovations, something that just does not happen at Rotary Club meetings. John McKeithen's growing appeal as a public officeholder for the national stage was never more in evidence than that day in Lafayette, Louisiana. Afterward, he leaned over to me and said, "Dave, your amendment is going to pass overwhelmingly. So is mine," he exulted.

Sure enough, on election day, Amendments #1 and #10 both won handily. I was astounded, but extremely gratified that #10 was the most popular of all amendments on the ballot, at 76 percent approval. In fact, it received more votes than any other measure in history at that point in time, as one of the fruits of that All Saints Day announcement by NFL commissioner Pete Rozelle, four years of effort by the New Orleans Pro Football Club, and the support of Governor McKeithen. John McKeithen said something the next day that I have never forgotten: "Dave, if motherhood were on the ballot, there would be at least 15 percent negative votes, so a 76 to 9 margin with responsible voters was truly remarkable."

It was on that day in late 1966 that I realized for certain John McKeithen was a political leader with outstanding national-office potential.

CHAPTER VII

The Fight for Our Dome

A unique and decisive Superdome experience came during early 1967 when I "sneaked," more or less, into the *Times-Picayune* building for a very private visit with Mr. John Tims, a good, honest man, then publisher of the *Times-Picayune* and the *New Orleans States-Item*. Tims, a tough, solid businessman who instituted business practices that would make the *Times-Picayune* a formidable economic success for years to come, was in direct contrast to The Editor. As I walked through the newsroom to meet Mr. Tims, I actually wore a disguise of sorts — horn-rimmed glasses at a time when I had never worn glasses a day in my life, plus other paraphernalia — all because I did not want to be recognized by anyone . . . and I do mean anyone! No one seemed to notice my coming or going, but of course, in later years, I realized that someone in the *Picayune* newsroom probably commented, "I didn't know Dave Dixon wears glasses."

During my visit with Mr. Tims, at one point, he opened his desk drawer and asked me to take a look. Inside was a gun! I thought to myself, "Why the hell is he showing me a gun? Does he think I'm some sort of threat to him?" Months later, I figured out that Mr. Tims could sense that I felt some concern for my personal safety in coming to see him. Maybe I had even said something to that effect. Through his gesture he was telling me that he didn't worry about his own safety, and this was his way of saying that he personally believed what I was telling him.

You see, I was about to become a very limited "whistle-blower," in a productive sense. The Superdome Commission, of which I was executive director and a board member by appointment of then Mayor Schiro, had begun to examine the credentials of architects and engineers, and Tims' remarkable response to my very private appeal for assistance played a huge role in preserving the Superdome's architectural integrity, assuring the fair selection of a gifted design architect.

My stealthy visit to the Picayune Tower had its roots in an early experience with John McKeithen. While still at the beginning of our Saints adventure, Mary and I had become personal friends with the McKeithen family. One day we received a telephone call from the governor stating that he would be making a political speech in St. Bernard Parish that evening. He asked if we would be available to keep him company on that drive. Of course we said yes.

Our ride to St. Bernard took us past the corner of Poydras and Claiborne, the location he, Mary, and I knew by then would be the ultimate site of the Superdome. I sensed that McKeithen was under pressure to appoint architectural and engineering firms that had been campaign contributors to himself, Mayor Schiro, Jefferson Parish president Tom Donelon, and perhaps other members of the Superdome commission. So as we passed Poydras and South Claiborne, I said, "You know, Governor, I have learned one thing for sure about architecture. It's unlike football, where there are dozens of 'upsets' every week. There are no upsets in architecture. Great architects build great buildings; good architects build good buildings; mediocre architects design mediocre buildings."

I continued, "This building, located at such a commanding site, right in our Central Business District, simply screams for a great architect. Your grandchildren and mine will curse the day both of us were born if some kind of ugly, inefficient abomination is built here. Whatever you choose to do, I'll support it, but I consider it essential that the selection of architects and engineers be based on merit, rather than political considerations. Almost every great firm in America is interested in this project, so we'll have lots of very talented people to consider." The governor didn't say a word, and I briefly thought I had offended him. But somehow I sensed that I had struck a chord, a formidable one, so I dropped the subject.

I didn't have to wait long. The next morning John McKeithen telephoned me at home about 6 A.M.: "Dave, what would you think of a committee of deans of Architecture and Engineering from Tulane and LSU to advise us on our selection of architects and engineers?"

We came up with a committee of three deans: Roger Richardson, dean of Engineering at LSU and for many years prior the chief of engineering for the vast Exxon complex just outside Baton Rouge; Gerald McLendon, the dean of LSU's School of Environmental Design; and John Lawrence, the dean of Architecture at Tulane. Very, very astute, outstanding gentlemen, all three of them.

Before presenting the committee to the commissioners, McKeithen asked me what I knew of John Lawrence, the Tulane dean of Architecture. I replied, "First class in every respect, talented, impeccably honest, a straight arrow." In turn I asked him about the LSU people. Ever the humorist, he replied, "Outstanding. Straight arrows also, painfully so." We both laughed, and from that moment on, I knew that John McKeithen was not only brilliant but a straight arrow himself . . . and that we were heading for an extremely exciting project that would make the people of Louisiana proud.

As for the site, full credit must go to Gulf South Research Institute's Ned Cole, one of their top researchers who early on spotted the Poydras Street property and knew instantly that he had hit the jackpot, the absolutely perfect site. When Ned presented his recommendation, first to McKeithen and then to me, we both knew that the location was spectacular and far surpassed all potential sites. The deans agreed unanimously. I believe, too, that Moon Landrieu, then a councilman, had a heavy hand here.

The deans were confirmed by the board of commissioners as an advisory group, and they moved into action almost immediately. I sat in on virtually all their meetings in order to keep the governor abreast of what was going on and to educate myself a bit as well as to advise them on occasion. This experience with the deans made me proud of our two great universities, and humanity in general. Within two weeks I knew their recommendations would be based strictly on the abilities of the architectural and engineering firms.

Col. Tom Bowen, a retired colonel from the U.S. Army Corps of Engineers, came on board as a technical adviser to the commission. Tom was very helpful to the commission and to the deans, as was his successor, Col. Mark Carrigan, also a retired Army Engineering colonel. Colonel Carrigan remained with the Superdome all the way through the completion date, then retired to San Antonio, where he now lives. Both were invaluable, impeccably honest, and extremely conscientious, as later was Mr. Tom Sutter, possessing years of invaluable executive experience with a major construction contractor. He served with marvelous efficiency as an overseer of construction along with Colonel Carrigan.

Eventually, the deans and our commission members narrowed the selection of architects and engineers to two top firms, Curtis & Davis of New Orleans and the Chicago office of the famous international firm Skidmore, Owings, and Merrill, two excellent choices. Both great firms committed their top design architects, including John Merrill of Skidmore, Owings, and Merrill, and Nathaniel C. Curtis, Jr., of Curtis & Davis. Mr. Curtis and Mr. Merrill made their firms' presentations in person. I'm not certain that I have met a more impressive person than John Merrill, head of Skidmore's Chicago office, but N.C. Curtis, Jr., chief design architect of Curtis & Davis, was every inch his equal.

Apparently the deans agreed with me because they recommended both the Skidmore firm and Curtis & Davis. The deans nominated Nathaniel C. "Buster" Curtis, Jr., as design architect over the nationally respected John Merrill because, as the deans said, "Everyone knows that Buster Curtis is a genius. Just look around the city at his work, and besides, being local, he will always be readily available." The governor strictly followed the deans' advice and recommended both firms, again specifying Buster Curtis as chief of design. In such a circumstance, when denied the design assignment, a top national firm such as Skidmore, Owings, and Merrill usually withdraws, and they did.

Skidmore, Owings, and Merrill had allied themselves with two local firms, Edward Silverstein and Associates and Nolan, Norman, and Nolan. A few days later the Silverstein and Nolan firms indicated that they would like to continue their association with the Superdome. This was welcome news to all of us, who were well aware of their talents and integrity. I had known both Ulisse Nolan and Eddie Silverstein for many years, perhaps a bit longer and better than I had known Buster Curtis.

All three New Orleans-based firms adapted well to their duties. Nolan and Silverstein were involved more with production papers and the all-important preparation of working prints, whereas Mr. Curtis handled design work and overall responsibility. They did a superb job of working together, but make no mistake, Buster Curtis was the key, essential person architecturally. The Superdome was his personal triumph.

Looking at our magnificent Superdome today, it is easy to see that Buster Curtis was a genius. I should add that he was also one of the finest individuals I have known. Mary and I are fond of Buster's business partner, Arthur Davis, and Arthur's wife, Mary. Unfortunately, Arthur was involved in other activities at the time and did not participate in the Superdome project. He is sometimes mistakenly identified as the Superdome's architect, which is erroneous because he had no involvement. Architecturally, our Louisiana Superdome is 100 percent Buster Curtis's building, a monumental accomplishment.

Well before the architects were selected, however, I had told *Picayune* publisher John Tims that it was predictable, and already visible, that the governor and all political office holders on the Board of Commissioners would be under huge pressure from their political contributors. I also stated that a front-page news story almost certainly would be available if a competent reporter were to visit with the three deans. By that time I knew that they would recommend architectural appointment on merit, and merit only in all respects.

Sure enough, Walter Cowan, a universally respected editor for the *New Orleans States,* undoubtedly designated by Mr. Tims, interviewed the three deans. Almost immediately they stated that they would resign their status with the Superdome commission if they thought that the selection of architects and engineers would be based on campaign contributions. The *States'* front-page headline was, "Deans Threaten to Resign." That

Dave Dixon and Buster Curtis display the Superdome model, 1967.

headline and accompanying story, perhaps more than any one event, solidified selection of architects and engineers by merit. Tims and Cowan struck solid blows on behalf of integrity. We were on our way to a building worthy of the title "Superdome."

After the article appeared, I remember the governor remarking that the commission would "dare not" (I loved that phrase) involve patronage in any decisions regarding the selection of architects and engineers, not with "those deans" and the newspapers looking on. A carefully couched comment, I thought.

Later, at a cocktail party I overheard the governor remark to one of his biggest political supporters, the head of a competent architectural firm (but one that was not well suited for a project of the Superdome's scope), "Those damned deans." At that moment I could not have been more proud of John McKeithen, nor more in admiration of his political skills. I watched him retain his political supporter while doing exactly the right thing by the people of Louisiana.

One day at his home in Columbia the governor asked, smiling somewhat wickedly, I thought, "Dave, you didn't have anything to do with that front-page newspaper story about the deans, did you?" I'd had a couple of months by then to supply the right political answer: "John, I remember well your telephone call to me suggesting that we form a committee of deans to help us with our selection of architects and engineers, but you don't think I would politically involve those great gentlemen in any way, do you? Especially since they were appointed by our governor." He roared with laughter and said, "Touché." We shook hands.

The Worldwide Appeal of the Saints

After the appointment of Curtis & Davis as the chief architectural firm and their selection (or inclusion) of Sverdrup & Parcel of St. Louis as construction and design engineers, this team of architects and engineers wanted to include my idea of "instant replay," but no team member was absolutely certain of the feasibility or the technology for such a feature. It did not exist anywhere—another first for our Superdome.

However, a celebrated Hollywood filmmaker (the head of Universal Studios) had told the governor and me during a meeting at his Hollywood headquarters that the famous Dutch electronics giant, Philips, had developed techniques and procedures that seemed to confirm the feasibility of giant-screen TV. It was deemed that I would go to the Philips Laboratories in Zurich, Switzerland, to see for myself, joined by a Sverdrup & Parcel electronics engineer. I wanted Mary, always my best adviser, to see this phenomenon, so I arranged to pay her airfare and all expenses out of our family's personal funds to witness a moment of triumph, or to help me wipe the egg off my face.

At Philips' Zurich Laboratories it was confirmed through tests, to the complete satisfaction of our engineer and myself, that revolutionary giant-screen instant replay would be available to Superdome football fans. We were elated, overjoyed, and proud that our Superdome would be the first stadium location in the world to enjoy this unique development, which, of course, was the forerunner to today's "There's a question on the play."

After Switzerland, Mary and I went to Austria, to the charming Alpine city of Salzburg, where we were entertained by the best yodeling group we have ever heard or seen in action, all equipped with Alpine horns of various types, all able to produce music of sorts. One yodeler introduced what he called "the longest Alpine horn in the world," perhaps twelve feet in length. Our man yodeled for a while, then actually pecked away at this "longest Alpine horn," finally producing music that was unmistakably "When the Saints Go Marching In." Mary and I almost fell out of our chairs at hearing this New Orleans favorite in a tiny Austrian nightclub, tucked away in some of the most beautiful, snow-packed mountains in the world. After a while the whole place began to swing to Alpine horns blasting away "When the Saints Go Marching In," some nine thousand miles away from our great city, where I had thought the song was created.

From Salzburg we went on to Rome, where a wonderful Dominican monsignor, Father Said, a friend of Mary's strongly Catholic family in Memphis, took us in tow at the Vatican. Though I was then a non-Catholic, we even participated in a grand audience with Pope Paul VI, along with two or three hundred others, including a delightful, giggling group of sixty young French nuns. They had taken their vows only the day before and were leaving the next day as missionaries to Brazil.

In a touching, memorable scene these cute French teenagers began to serenade their pope in French as Paul VI passed before them. So help me, there was no question that they were singing "When the Saints Go Marching In," in French, the best sounding language in the world to these ears. I turned to our Dominican host, explaining the popularity in our city of this wonderful little hymn, so much so that we had named our already famous New Orleans Saints football team after the song. Our monsignor, French himself, went on to state that this beautiful little song originated in the sixteenth century as a French hymn. When I returned home, officials at the Historic New Orleans Jazz Club confirmed the sixteenth-century origin as fact.

Two days in a row we had heard "When the Saints Go Marching In" being sung, in Austria and then in Rome. Mary and I did not expect anyone to believe us, but those things are precisely what happened on these little side trips, both within forty-eight hours of our triumph in inventing, in effect, stadium instant replay in Zurich.

As was Mary's trip to Zurich, the trips to Salzburg and Vatican City were expensed from personal funds, perhaps frustrating one or two critics (ah, The Editor!) in our home city who might have hoped to embarrass me and my family. We beat them again. Or, as Franklin Roosevelt said, "Again and again and again."

It was a great trip. Lots of Saints. Upon our return we felt great about our city's NFL future, not knowing that a major difficulty lay immediately and unexpectedly ahead.

John Schwegmann

An unexpected obstacle to our Superdome, a formidable adversary, emerged in early 1967 after voter approval of the constitutional amendment that created the Louisiana Stadium and Exposition District, the Superdome executive body. That obstacle's name was John Schwegmann, the eccentric multimillionaire grocer and national pioneer in supermarkets. Schwegmann operated several Giant Super Markets, including a huge facility that was the largest in America at one point. Dating almost from the opening of his first market in the 1940s, Schwegmann bought adjacent two-page ads in the *Picayune* every day and placed at the top of the centerfold a box measuring approximately 5 x 8 inches containing his personal views on various political and social matters, always written clearly, powerfully, and forcefully. In short order he had become a political force.

He used the political notoriety he gained to win an election bid for the Louisiana Senate. As Senate approval for Superdome legislation loomed, I talked to state senator Schwegmann at his desk on the Senate floor. He stated his support of the Superdome project, and later that day in early 1967 he voted for the legislation, so he was originally supportive. Senator Schwegmann would afterward deny that he had voted in favor of the Superdome, but I know what I saw, heard, and read at that crucial legislative session. Knowing that he had voted in favor of Superdome legislation, I was astounded when via his *Picayune* advertising he later launched attack after attack on the Superdome and its general concept, lasting from 1967 through 1968 and into 1969.

By the 1960s, John Schwegmann's stores were making millions of dollars buying direct from distillers and selling various brands of wines, whiskey, and beer at low, low prices. A brilliant young lawyer named Paul Pigman, associated with the distinguished law firm of Stone, Pigman, Walther, Wittman, known then as Wisdom and Stone, had become nationally famous for defeating the state's fair-trade law, which had allowed prices for an entire region to be set by a manufacturer in contract with only one area retailer. The defeat of that law enabled Schwegmann stores to buy directly from distillers, thereby permitting him to reduce his prices and making his Giant Super Markets widely popular. John Schwegmann could hardly open new locations quickly enough.

Bolstered by the success of the fair-trade litigation,

Schwegmann confidently set out to tackle the Superdome. His talented lawyer, Phil Wittman, Stone, Pigman's top litigator, and the best I have seen, actually won the first lawsuit filed against the Stadium Commission in the court of Judge Oliver "Ike" Carriere, later overturned. Eventually our Superdome attorneys won twenty-two of twenty-three cases with the one loss reversed, including a final, and decisive, victory in the State Supreme Court. With that State Supreme Court verdict, a huge victory for Louisiana and our attorney Harry B. Kelleher, at long last the Superdome was on its way. There were no further lawsuits.

However, the attacks from state senator Schwegmann continued, and no one, including the governor, could figure out what was motivating him. He seemed confused and erratic. Why was he doing these things? After all, the Superdome game was over. Moreover, the huge bond issue to support financing of the Superdome's construction had been sold in May 1970.

At that point I was nursing a sore back that required long hot-bath sessions. One morning my brilliant wife, Mary, called to me while I was enjoying a hot tub: "I know why John Schwegmann is giving us so much trouble. He's going to run for governor."

"Ho, ho, ho," I laughed. But my laughter died down gradually as I began to comprehend what John Schwegmann was doing, and I soon realized that Mary, as usual, was correct. I finally said, "Sweetheart, you are dead right. Of course, that's what he's doing. He figures that with his huge advertising account the *Times-Picayune,* including The Editor, will never attack him, even though our community would be the loser from his actions. And with his daily political ads, 100 percent tax deductible with his so-called editorials included as part of his grocery ads, he can convince enough people in the New Orleans area to vote for him against their own best interest of not putting the NFL and the Superdome at risk."

"He also figures," Mary added, "that he'll be popular with the Baton Rouge media and in north Louisiana, and that he'll be a strong candidate."

"You are 100 percent correct. Hand me the phone, please," I replied. I called Governor McKeithen right away, and he went through the same procedure as I. His laughter faded as he said, "Tell Mary she's right. Of course, he's running for governor in 1972. But your governor will take care of John 'Schwegermann' very shortly. I'm speaking to the regional convention of the Southern Baptists in Shreveport next week." At this point McKeithen was well into his second term and could not run again.

Indeed, our governor did "take care" of Senator "Schwegermann." He always pronounced the Schwegmann name with an extra "er." Speaking to a Southern Baptist convention, John McKeithen's first words were: "John Schwegermann actually might make a fine governor. He's so rich, you know, that he could finance his own campaign and not be obligated to anybody. For many years until U.S. senator Estes Kefauver shut him down about ten years ago, he had huge revenues from those ninety-eight slot machines in that big old Giant Super Market of his down there in N'awlins.

"And since he won that big anti-trust lawsuit so that he can buy direct from the huge distilleries, I understand that he has become the largest liquor dealer in the world. He has such tremendous cash reserves from those old slot machines and those huge wine, whiskey, and beer profits, millions of dollars a month, that he can finance his own campaign."

Our governor told me that a hush fell over that assembly of five thousand Southern Baptists when he described Schwegmann as "the largest liquor dealer in the world." "I think Senator Schwegermann's campaign for governor might be over before he can even get started," John McKeithen pronounced to Mary and me.

Sure enough, the "Schwegermann" campaign for governor folded quickly as John Schwegmann took a good look at the real world of politics. He admitted to me once that Mary's view of his plans to use the Superdome to help him become governor was accurate.

John Schwegmann was a very formidable adversary at one point. For some reason he and I never had cross words for each other. I did not admire his apparent willingness to shortchange New Orleans with his crude attempts to harm the Saints and destroy the Superdome in order to ingratiate himself to many upstate voters away from New Orleans and to stir up old animosities. But I did recognize the fact that he battled every day of his life, that he clawed, bit, kicked, chewed, and fought his way to the top of an impressive empire. Too bad he didn't channel all those energies and ambitions to something better than destroying his hometown's precious possessions in an effort to secure his way into the governor's mansion.

I actually enjoyed our little battles, particularly the two debates we had over Channel 12, WYES, in New Orleans, a PBS station. One rather remarkable exchange took place during our first debate. The moderator, not a WYES staff member, was so obviously in Schwegmann's employ that I turned on him on the air, live, and said, "Why don't you leave us alone and let Senator Schwegmann and me handle this debate ourselves? You're supposed to be neutral, which obviously you are not." John Schwegmann laughed—I had never seen him laugh before—and he and I had a good debate without the "neutral" moderator saying another word.

I've always thought that my adversary tried to fix the debate, got caught red-handed, and then laughed about it. I admired his ingenuity and resourcefulness. Imagine, fixing a debate. I'm proud of myself for spotting what was happening. I had progressed a bit from my very naïve early days.

At the end we shook hands, and he invited me to lunch the next day at his big Airline Highway store. We had a nice visit. I ended up liking John Schwegmann, and I felt for him when a later stroke took the fight out of him. He was a warrior, but also something of an unprincipled opportunist. John Schwegmann was the Wal-Mart of his day. I would not doubt that Sam Walton observed John Schwegmann in action and actually improved on the Schwegmann way of doing things. In fact, I'd bet on it.

CHAPTER VIII

A Tennis Interlude

During early to mid-1967, as we undertook the job of creating the organizational framework for future Superdome operations, I hired away from the Miami Dolphins as my chief assistant a magnificent young man named Bob Briner, who eventually went on to great achievements in the TV production industry and in tennis. Superbly intelligent, he was a fine human being who always abided by strong principles and ethics. He was highly, highly recommended by one of America's top sports editors, Edwin Pope of the *Miami Herald.* Bob Briner and I set about studying and conceiving future sports and entertainment events for the Superdome.

One thing that caught our eye was professional tennis, as compared to the then "shamateur" system employed by Wimbledon and the United States Tennis Association at Forest Hills, New York, in which the game's stars were paid generous "expenses" under the table. We saw almost immediately that the real future in tennis was not in the exhibition tours staged by top stars such as Jack Kramer and Pancho Gonzales during the 1950s and 1960s, and definitely not "shamateurism." Instead, all top players should be professionals, we believed, who would play weekly tournaments, much like the PGA in golf. That's what exists today in tennis.

My friend Lamar Hunt agreed with our theories. He and I formed World Championship Tennis, Inc. (WCT) during late 1967, owned equally by the two of us. To bring our tennis project into being, I was granted a leave of absence from my Superdome duties, though it was quite clear that McKeithen expected me back within a few months. In short order Lamar and I signed most of the top male players in the world to professional contracts, including all four Wimbledon semifinalists. Most of our signing bonuses were a tailor-made suit of clothes at Saville Row in London. That was the sad state of "big time" tennis in 1967.

Initially, Lamar and I had several objectives in mind for World Championship Tennis. Our first goal was to force tennis away from its "shamateur" practices in which so-called amateur players were paid under-the-table sums of money to compete in various tournaments. As we strove to achieve this aim, we signed virtually every top player in the world to a WCT contract.

It could be said that we immediately accomplished our first objective. I remember well the day that Sir Herman David, the chairman of the All England Tennis Club (Wimbledon) telephoned me to ask whether we would allow our players to compete if Wimbledon were to go to open tennis, in which players openly are paid various sums of money tied directly to performance. In other words, the largest sum would be won by the champion, with the runner-up receiving less money, exactly as in professional golf. Lamar and I agreed, of course, and thus was born the era of open tennis. It was rather incredible that such an important, historic change in the world structure of a great sport could be accomplished so quickly.

We also achieved our second objective. World Championship Tennis initiated a tie-breaker system that largely resembled the tie-breaker commonly used in today's tennis.

Our third aim, one that was mostly successful, was designed to help tennis fans. Prior to the WCT, all tournaments worldwide required each contestant to wear all-white clothes. It was our objective to designate that one player in each match wear a traditional all-white outfit. The other player would be required to wear a shirt of a distinctive solid color, whatever he might choose. A player could be identified by always wearing one particular color when designated, if he or she wished. This innovation would make it easy to identify the players at the blink of an eye. Tennis contestants change courts frequently and on a scheduled basis to even out conditions such as wind, sun, and court condition, sometimes making it difficult to distinguish who is who, on TV and in person.

In the 2005 Wimbledon Championship Final, for example, it was difficult at times to identify who was Roger Federer and who was Andy Roddick. To require one player to wear a distinctive, solid-color shirt would be simple to implement and would improve the fan's viewing experience, particularly when players are of similar size and other physical characteristics. Alas, tennis is still not very visionary. There should be absolute color rules.

Finally, we had hoped to convert tennis to a point system of scoring. The first player to win, say, 20 points by a 2-point margin would win a set. On this point we were unsuccessful. The traditions of "15-30-40-game" and the terms "love," "advantage," and "deuce" instead of scores of zero and "even" make tennis distinctive and add to the game's traditions and uniqueness. I, for one, agree now that the present game-set-match structure adds a special flavor to this magnificent sport. Our objective to change the scoring system was in error.

I do not know of a better spectator sport than when two closely matched tennis players are competing. Among major sports only prize fighting possesses this feature of one-on-one, but boxing is a primitive, brutal, unsafe "sport" that should be outlawed. Tennis is a very strenuous athletic competition when played at a championship level and requires top physical condition as much as basketball, for example. Tennis has everything in my opinion. However, it is the most underdeveloped spectator and participant sport in the world. In popularity and potential tennis is still in its infancy.

Though the WCT was not able to impact all aspects of the sport, one of the really nice dividends of conceiving and organizing World Championship Tennis with Lamar was the fact that the tennis tour created circumstances that enabled Mary and me to become close friends with Randy and Isabel Gregson, a grand New Orleans couple. We became regular visitors to Wimbledon for several years, even after I had sold my share of the WCT to my partner, Lamar Hunt. Wimbledon is a delightful experience, well worth a special trip and visit to London, even for those who are not great tennis fans. The Wimbledon atmosphere is superb.

We were so proud of Randy Gregson when he became president

of the United States Tennis Association, Wimbledon's American counterpart. As such, Randy's Wimbledon tickets were for the Royal Box, theoretically reserved for the queen, always occupied by nobility and, of course, our humble, modest, dignified friend from Camp Street, New Orleans' J. Randolph Gregson. It always thrilled me to glance toward the Royal Box and witness our distinguished friend conversing freely with nobility. Actually, J. Randolph, whom I had known for years as plain "Randy," once confided to me that he felt that this was his purpose in life, that he had been born for such a role, that he enjoyed giving his views on affairs of state and the world to England's House of Windsor.

One day I momentarily glanced away from a magnificent duel between the German phenom, Boris Becker, and one of the great Swedish stars to check on my friend, the Duchess of Kent, and other nobility. I was totally unprepared for what I saw. There was J. Randolph Gregson, the nice guy from refined, aristocratic, Uptown New Orleans, actually the Garden District, with his head slumped badly to his right and his jaws wide open, obviously in deep slumber, amidst the immediate proximity of royalty. Did he snore?

I immediately called to my wife, "Mary, the camera, quickly!" (Sort of like boyhood days, "Quick, Henry, the Flit" to exterminate threatening mosquitoes.) I took several shots of Super Randolph, as I had always called him before and after his royal sleep. The negative still rests in our safe deposit box.

I have given my word to J. Randolph's wonderful wife, Isabel, that I shall never embarrass Randy by showing prints of her husband's famous slumber to mutual friends in the Uptown New Orleans cocktail and dinner party set, or, heaven forbid, sending this memorable snapshot of Super Randy, New Orleans' president of the United States Tennis Association, to *Tennis Magazine* or *Sports Illustrated.*

So help me, his jaw appeared to bealmost dislocated! My word, how wide can a jaw droop? J. Randolph had just set a new world's record for a drooped jaw. Actually, Randy Gregson has given thousands of hours of service and dedication to this great sport. He should be in the national Tennis Hall of Fame at Newport, Rhode Island, but at least I ensured that he was recognized properly by our Louisiana Sports Hall of Fame in 2005.

Another very amusing incident initiated, in a sense, our World Championship Tennis Tour. We were to open the tour in Australia, and I asked Nicki Pilic, a 1967 Wimbledon semifinalist who had signed with us, to meet me in New Orleans, stay at our home for a few days, and participate in the Sugar Bowl Tennis Championships. The site was Fogelman Arena, then known as the Tulane Gym, an excellent indoor facility for tennis. The great Arthur Ashe was in the field, and the Sugar Bowl executives figured that Ashe and Pilic would make a spectacular final. We were, of course, very happy to help the Sugar Bowl.

This was in the dying days of "shamateurism," and Arthur Ashe was still an amateur, who had been paid nicely for his appearance. Naturally, the Sugar Bowl Tennis Championship was billed as an amateur event, so I counseled Nicki very carefully not to declare himself as a professional until after the Sugar Bowl competition. Imagine my surprise to read a brief Associated Press story datelined Split, Yugoslavia (Nicki's home town), announcing that Nicki Pilic had turned professional and would be joining the World Championship Tennis Tour to begin in Australia in January. I immediately telephoned Nicki at his home in Split and softly admonished him. Nicki said immediately, "Oh, is okay, when I get to New Orleans, if anybody ask, I deny press conference!"

I contacted the Sugar Bowl tennis chairman who immediately said, "Let's not say anything to anybody. Tell Nicki not to deny his announcement, just don't say anything to anybody. In tennis today the lines between 'pro' and 'amateur' are pretty much meaningless. Just say, 'No speak English.'"

So, the Sugar Bowl tournament went on. There were a number of excellent matches. Sure enough, Arthur Ashe and Nicki Pilic met in a spectacular five-set final with Arthur winning in the fifth set, 10 to 8. Numerous match points, both ways.

The crowd was standing room only, close to fifty-five hundred, easily the most exciting tennis match ever played in New Orleans to this day, according to virtually all my tennis friends, including the great J. Randolph Gregson, soon to consort with nobility, who counseled Nicki how to "deny Split press conference" in English, but only if called upon for an explanation. As we say in New Orleans on such occasions, "Nobody asked nobody nothing!" and there was no reason to deny the press conference.

From New Orleans and the highly successful Sugar Bowl Tennis Championship, Nicki, Mary and I, and our eleven-year-old son, Stuart, flew to Sydney, Australia, where our stable of eight top World Championship Tennis players met us for training and for a special ABC-TV championship tour televised in many parts of the world, eventually won by our John Newcombe, the reigning two-time Wimbledon champion.

We called our guys, who included four current Wimbledon semifinalists, the "Handsome Eight" because all really were quite good looking. There were John Newcombe and Tony Roche from Australia; Pierre Barthes, the number one Frenchman; Roger Taylor, Britain's number one player; Denis Ralston, from Bakersfield, California, America's number one; Cliff Drysdale, from South Africa; Earl "Butch" Buchholst, one of my favorites, a top American from St. Louis; and, of course, Nicki Pilic from Yugoslavia.

John Newcombe won that January 1968 opening event in Sydney and was mobbed by almost every cute young girl in Australia. Hysterical! The Handsome Eight were off to a grand start.

From Sydney we flew to Kansas City, where Lamar Hunt met us. The Kansas City tournament again was won by Newcombe. From there we set off for St. Louis, then Houston, New Orleans, and Miami. Great fun, great tennis, a different winner at each stop. Our guys were well-matched.

However, I soon realized that being away from Mary and our three young sons was no fun for me. I asked Bob Briner to step in temporarily as tour director. Eventually, Bob went on to a magnificent career in tennis management and in television production with Donald Dell, amassing a tidy fortune. I had selected well when I recruited this exceptional human being.

Meanwhile, as we were preparing to leave a successful stop

The Handsome Eight, 1979.

at Houston, I received a telephone call from Governor McKeithen. I was surprised that he sounded tired, almost dejected, not at all like the always affable, enthusiastic person Mary and I knew so well. He asked simply that both of us come to the Governor's Mansion in Baton Rouge some time during our upcoming stop at New Orleans. We were concerned, so we arranged to go to the mansion promptly. Almost immediately he asked me to return to the Superdome project "as soon as possible," that he "needed" me there. "Urgently," he said. I looked at Mary, she looked at me, and I accepted on the spot.

To this day I think he was reading my mind, or possibly Mary had contacted him expressing concern that the tour was wearing me down. Mostly, I think that he knew that I was "his man" at the Superdome and that I would keep him intimately informed of every development.

I decided to sell my half-interest in the WCT to my partner,

Lamar Hunt. Being away from home and wife and young children was simply not my cup of English tea, so Mary and I decided that I would end any leave of absence and return to the Superdome as executive director. I knew that the enormously capable Bob Briner could take over my WCT duties full-time and that my departure from the WCT almost certainly would be amicable (which it proved to be in all respects). Though my time with World Championship Tennis was abbreviated, I am proud to have had at least a small influence on the sport, and I am certain that my friends Lamar Hunt and Bob Briner feel the same way about their own involvement.

With tennis behind me, I refocused my energies on Louisiana. I knew John McKeithen, and I sensed that something else was eating at him. Soon enough, I was to discover at least a part of the reason.

A Tennis Ball

Before leaving the subject of tennis, I would like to share a joke told to me by former Louisiana governor Edwin Edwards. At the time, Edwards had recently beaten David Duke in the gubernatorial election. We met one afternoon for lunch and after he showed me his election poll, we walked over to Mena's Palace in the French Quarter. On the way he told me one of the funniest jokes I have heard in a lifetime, perhaps so amusing because of his wonderful patois.

Edwards said, "This guy had been playing tennis in one of your downtown tennis clubs. When he finished playing, he walked along Royal Street carrying his tennis racquet, with one tennis ball in his right side pocket and one in his back pocket.

"A friend rushed up to him, saying, 'Jim, I've been looking for you all morning. I'm having a luncheon at Galatoire's today with some really delightful visitors. You've got to join us, you'll be the twelfth and final person. I'll get you a jacket to wear; Galatoire's has a big selection of them at the door.'" At that time, jackets were mandatory at Galatoire's.

"Eventually Jim accepted. Directly across from Jim at the end of the table was a super attractive gal from California named Jane. Finally, Jane said, 'My curiosity is killing me. What in the world is that bulge in your right side pocket?' Jim replied, 'Oh, that's a tennis ball.' She seemed shocked, then replied, 'A tennis ball? I knew you could have a tennis elbow, but a tennis ball, my goodness. Are you serious? Doesn't it hurt?'"

When Governor Edwards finished his joke, I was laughing so hard that I almost fell down.

A couple of months later a distinguished-looking gentleman, an out-of-towner, was visiting my gallery on Royal Street, and I ended up telling him the Tennis Ball joke. He laughed just as hard as I and said, "I can't tell you how perfect is the timing of that joke. The International Society of Urologists, as you know, twenty thousand strong, is meeting in New Orleans this week. I am the president of our National Academy, and I have to address five hundred of the top urologists in the world at a black-tie dinner this evening. I'm going to open my talk with your Tennis Ball joke. It is the perfect urological joke."

This distinguished, internationally known physician returned the next day especially to thank me, saying, "Your governor's Tennis Ball joke was a tremendous hit, arousing more laughter than I've ever heard at one of our meetings. You've made me famous worldwide, and I'm grateful to you. Everyone said that it was absolutely the perfect joke for a meeting of urologists!" Which I guess it was.

CHAPTER IX

President
John J. McKeithen

The story of my lifetime in New Orleans, though largely an autobiography, shows how my personal experiences affected the creation of the Saints and our Louisiana Superdome. The sum of those experiences created the close, intimate spectator's view that Mary and I had of events that I believe changed the political landscape of America. I am ready now to tell the amazing story of "The Scandal" and how, believe it or not, our greatest Louisiana governor, John J. McKeithen, nearly became vice president of the United States of America in 1969 and, conceivably, could have become president in 1977. Only four persons living today know the facts you are about to read. As a courtesy, I have telephoned the other witnesses, and they agreed that it is time to share the full story.

I have voted sixteen times in national elections, ten times for one party, six times for the other. I vote for whomever I believe to be the better candidate. A rare bird today in a politically polarized America, I consider myself a moderate, as I know was my great friend, John McKeithen. Therefore, do not label how I am going to describe the political facts of 1967-68 as I saw them at that time and still see them today.

Time-Life, the great publishing giant, misled unintentionally, I am quite willing to say, its readers and the people of America through an oddly timed series of *Life* articles during September 1967. Those 1967 *Life* stories profoundly affected the outcome of the 1968 presidential election in favor of the tragic Richard Milhous Nixon and his equally sad hand-picked running mate, Spiro T. Agnew.

But, first, let's set the national political stage as it existed during early fall 1967. Things were not going all that well in

Vietnam; indeed, I seem to recall that there emerged the first faint speculation that an embattled Pres. Lyndon Johnson might not stand for reelection in 1968. I had been shocked to learn from John McKeithen sometime during 1967 that he believed privately President Johnson would *not* run in 1968. He said, "The president looks tired, very tired." He seems to know something, I thought. Just as major corporations, businesses, and industries consider a myriad of future contingencies, so do political parties and elected officials at all levels, particularly the national political parties and their officeholders. In retrospect, I recognize that Lyndon Johnson's decision in March 1968 not to seek reelection as president could not have been a tremendous surprise to any political insider. His announcement was huge news but not a monumental surprise, not to sitting vice president Hubert Humphrey, not to Robert Kennedy, not to Richard Nixon—and certainly not to John McKeithen. Even more likely, some would say, not to Time-Life. However, *Life* and others said that they were shocked and stunned at the decision, inferring great surprise. It would be safe to state that every one of those players had factored in the possibility of a Lyndon Johnson withdrawal. Any sensible political planner would have done so.

In such an event the logical choice of the Democratic Party for its 1968 presidential nomination would be Vice Pres. Hubert H. Humphrey, ever a party loyalist and scrupulously loyal to his president. Humphrey understandably would have indulged in at least a little bit of his own fantasizing, perhaps as early as late July and early August 1967, including the very private consideration of a range of possible running mates. The ideal, of course, would be the "perfect" Southern Moderate, a charismatic campaigner, someone who could counter decisively Nixon's already announced "Southern Strategy."

By the spring of 1967, Nixon, the vice president under Dwight D. Eisenhower and 1960 presidential candidate, was openly seeking the 1968 Republican presidential nomination, proclaiming publicly his so-called Southern Strategy by which with cleverly phrased racial code words he hoped to break the old Solid South grip of the Democratic party. A successful Southern Strategy could deal a lethal, near-mortal blow to the Democrats and propel Nixon straight into the White House. So the existence of a Southern Moderate as a running mate would be a gift from heaven for candidate Humphrey.

That gift from heaven clearly would have been John McKeithen, easily the most attractive Southern Moderate in high office. Enormously popular, by late 1967 he was a political leader of considerable skill and accomplishment after having been elected governor in late 1963 and reelected overwhelmingly in 1967. McKeithen was a tremendous campaigner who spoke the Southern "language" perhaps better than anyone. He also had national appeal; he could go anywhere and speak expertly and with authority on almost any topic of national or international concern. No question, he would have won votes for Humphrey nationwide. Handsome, with rugged good looks, still built like an LSU halfback, he was also a superb, almost heroic orator (the best I have heard in a lifetime). John McKeithen had charisma, which would have made him a "star," not just in the south, but everywhere. I know that there was contact between Humphrey and McKeithen during that summer and at other times, including a publicized Humphrey visit to Baton Rouge in April 1968. I also remember that McKeithen and Humphrey disappeared together for more than an hour at the Washington Mardi Gras of 1967, McKeithen telling me later, "It was just politics, but very interesting."

John McKeithen as a Democratic vice-presidential candidate might have persuaded a third-party candidate, Alabama governor George Wallace, whom he knew well, not to run for president in 1968. It was widely rumored that Wallace had stated to McKeithen that he would withdraw his candidacy in the face of a Humphrey-McKeithen ticket, thereby creating an old-fashioned Democratic landslide. This would have been a giant step toward preserving the Solid South and the famous "Yellow Dog" Democrats for the Democratic Party.

Mary and I were visiting the McKeithens at their home in Columbia, Louisiana, on one occasion in 1967 when he received a call from Governor Wallace. Immediately afterward I was surprised (shocked, actually) to hear John McKeithen say, "You know something, I've never believed George Wallace is a

Gov. John McKeithen, Vice Pres. Hubert Humphrey, and Sen. Russell Long, 1967.

Hubert Humphrey and Mary and Dave Dixon at Mardi Gras Ball, 1967.

racist." He then described Wallace as "probably a populist who realized that to be elected governor of Alabama during the 1960s he must at least sound like a racist." Sad history, but logical. "In his private comments to me he has never sounded like a racist, and I can smell one a mile away," McKeithen continued. "That would explain his famous statement, made privately to a friend after losing a close governor's race to 'Kissing Jim' Folsom, that 'they'll never out-nigger George Wallace again.'" McKeithen then said, "I know him from Southern Governors' Conferences. We get along well," all of which surprised me greatly.

If McKeithen in Hubert Humphrey's private ruminations seemed to be the perfect running mate, think how he must have looked to Richard Nixon. Republican insiders had to have realized that McKeithen could weaken or ruin Nixon's Southern Strategy. Time-Life was then considered by many to be a traditionally Republican-leaning media outlet. After all, their publisher and absolute boss was Henry Luce, thought to be a Republican, the husband of Claire Booth Luce, a noted Republican diplomat and a highly regarded individual. As a personal friend of mine who knew the Luces well, both professionally and socially, declared, "Publisher Henry Luce could not be openly partisan, but, believe me, any man married to Claire Booth Luce would be strongly Republican."

It probably was coincidental, but *Life* began a series of exposés dated September 1, 8, and 29, 1967, supposedly linking Gov. John McKeithen to the extinct, or almost-extinct, New Orleans mafia, which had "gone legitimate," to the New York mafia, or possibly even to the Alaskan mafia. *Life* did not seem to know anything about the alleged mafia ties except that one Aubrey Young, a likable person but described by insiders in the Louisiana governor's office as a ninth-string gofer with a drinking problem, apparently introduced in January 1967 "a New York friend of a New Orleans friend" to one Edward Grady Partin. Partin was head of the Baton Rouge teamsters and it was his 1966 testimony that had sent Jimmy Hoffa, the notorious national teamsters president, to jail and out of office. *Life* alleged that both the New York teamsters and the New York mafia wanted Hoffa out of jail and back in office as teamsters president.

Oddly, this January event was not reported by *Life* until September 1, 1967, eight months after the fact. This alleged link to McKeithen was a non-story until the governor began to emerge in close circles as a Democratic vice-presidential possibility.

During that January 1967 introduction Aubrey allegedly overheard a one-million-dollar bribe being offered to Partin by the New York visitor so that he would recant his testimony against Hoffa. Horrified at what he had stumbled into, Aubrey reportedly went on a three-day drinking binge, then returned to work and blurted out his experience to Governor McKeithen, who fired him on the spot (later allowing him to resign) and reportedly called the FBI. To his credit Partin declined the offer and reportedly notified the Justice Department promptly.

On this flimsy basis, a September 1, 1967, *Life* exposé linked McKeithen to the New Orleans mafia, describing Aubrey Young as "an aide and confidant of Governor McKeithen." By its third article on September 29, *Life* had promoted Aubrey to a "key assistant and confidant." Those four little words, "key assistant and confidant," are so ridiculously inaccurate as to represent incredible ineptness for such a world-famous publisher. The references to Young as a confidant caused much laughter, and yes, considerable anger in McKeithen inner circles and among his office staff. Aubrey Young's main duty was to serve as a gofer or occasional chauffer, when sober, for the governor's guests or visitors (such as Mary Dixon and I). Even Aubrey's close friends described him as a likable, recovering alcoholic who was not doing a very good job of recovering, nothing close to a governor's confidant.

Life's claim was a careless stretch, as true and accurate as saying that George Washington, the father of our country, was mafia influenced. However, those three 1967 *Life* stories must have convinced Hubert Humphrey that his best choice in 1968 for a vice-presidential running mate, Louisiana governor John J. McKeithen, was connected to, or influenced by, a New Orleans mafia that likely no longer existed by September 1967. The national magazine carelessly intruded into the politics of America, making some scandalous mistakes in 1967 and 1968 that hurt our country badly and wronged a great man.

Even today "mafia" must be the worst word in the world for a presidentially minded person to hear about himself or any associate. It obviously scared the hell out of Hubert Humphrey, who eventually chose Ed Muskie as his running mate instead of the "perfect" McKeithen. Muskie helped to carry Maine but was of little political value nationally, and Richard Nixon carried the old Solid Democratic South, which went Republican for the first time since the Civil War. This created a true disaster for the Democrats, one that persists today. Nixon won a close election by six-tenths of one percentage point from Humphrey, and the Southern states, with a few Wallace votes elsewhere, would have meant the difference. This was just what the Republicans wanted. McKeithen wouldn't have carried one or two Southern states, he'd have carried all of them and made a chump out of Nixon, not a racist but quite willing to play the race card for political gain. Incredibly, "key assistant and confidant," those four erroneous words, colossal exaggerations, changed Louisiana history, American history, and world history — all for the worse. Humphrey would have gotten us out of Vietnam, and McKeithen would have been very, very popular as a Democrat who delivered the old Solid South in 1968 and key votes elsewhere, a superb campaigner, the perfect running mate for reelection in 1972. Ironically, both Nixon and Agnew committed criminal acts while in office, leading to their departure, so these men were not model citizens benefiting from Time-Life's claims concerning McKeithen's alleged illicit connections.

During these crucial months of 1967, I was on leave from Superdome duties, largely occupied with the World Championship Tennis lineup, which involved considerable overseas travel and absence from Louisiana. We did not subscribe to *Life* magazine at our home or office, so I did not see immediately, nor get to scrutinize, the three critical articles printed by *Life* that September. I didn't even hear about them until a bit later. Consequently, I did not realize the extent of what *Life* was doing, even if unintentionally, to John McKeithen; otherwise, I would have screamed "foul" at the top of my voice. The moment I would have seen the words "key assistant and confidant" used by *Life* to describe Aubrey Young, I am absolutely certain that I would have rushed to the defense of John McKeithen. I knew firsthand from frequent visits to the governor's office in Baton Rouge, the Governor's Mansion, and his home in Columbia, Louisiana, that Aubrey was no key assistant and absolutely not a confidant.

Aubrey Young was a likable person who, aside from battling an acute addiction to alcohol, suffered from the demons of deep depression and distress, which in fairness could affect anyone's judgment. He was from the Monroe area, twenty miles from Columbia, Louisiana, the McKeithen ancestral home. Though Aubrey was a good person in many ways, he blundered into a disaster, which any competent reporter should have recognized.

Out of kindness McKeithen had given Aubrey a job in his office as little more than a "glorified gofer," according to Gus Weill, a noted author and a key McKeithen campaign consultant and adviser. Also, according to everyone from Mary Evelyn Parker, then the distinguished, longtime state treasurer of Louisiana, to Rita Vicknair, the governor's secretary, and Edna Tingle, a lifelong family friend and manager of the governor's law office in Columbia, all legitimate confidants of the governor, Aubrey Young was nothing close to being a key figure in McKeithen's office, as *Life* stated so incorrectly to the American public.

Life never identified who contacted Aubrey Young for an introduction and meeting with Edward Grady Partin, head of the Baton Rouge teamsters. Nor did the magazine ever say who visited with Mr. Partin, allegedly to present him with a million-dollar bribe to recant the testimony that had sent Jimmy Hoffa to jail. Young apparently knew Partin, either by prior employment or as a casual drinking partner, or both. *Life* does allege that Young introduced an alleged New York visitor to Partin, who allegedly rejected the alleged bribe offer and allegedly telephoned the Justice Department. The magazine had lots of allegations, but *Life* did not seem to know anything definitively. Did the Partin bribery attempt even occur? There is no way to be sure, judging from *Life*'s apparent carelessness.

McKeithen was such a decent man he must not have recognized what was happening to him. Instead, he thought it was all a misunderstanding that he could rectify by visiting *Life*'s managing editor and reporters in person to let them see what an honest, sincere person they had wrongly linked in their guilt-by-association articles. This example of over self-confidence was the only political mistake I knew John McKeithen to make in his entire political career, but it was a huge mistake.

Had I been present (I was in Johannesburg, I believe), I am certain that I would have counseled my friend not to visit *Life* under any circumstances. Their ultimate choice of words to describe Aubrey was a dead giveaway that either they had other motives or were a terribly inept, dangerously careless magazine (at least on this one major political story). It is curious that no indictments materialized, even though the FBI was listening closely, J. Edgar Hoover having had all the phones in the Governor's Mansion tapped in order to look for "dirt" as McKeithen rose in national prominence. The correct course for John McKeithen might have been to visit very privately with Hubert Humphrey and explain the situation to him. Humphrey was a very intelligent man who, skillfully using the power of the vice presidency, could have turned this nonsense to his strong advantage. Also a reasonable man, he could have found an agreeable solution if *Life*'s motives were also reasonable.

We'll never know for sure, but if it looks like a duck, walks like a duck, and quacks like a duck, it must be mafia, or so *Life* magazine scandalously tried to convince its reading public in 1967. Do I believe that *Life* participated in a conspiracy? Definitely not. Time-Life had too much to lose to participate in what would have been a totally bizarre plot. In my view a great institution simply had a rare moment of carelessness, pettiness, and incompetence, even if that lets the publication off the hook it so willingly and inexcusably swallowed.

The publication's mistakes began with the writer it allowed to write the exposés. All three *Life* articles were attributed to a "Sandy Smith," whose writing style is strongly suggestive of a part-time, "stories for sale" writer named David Chandler. This New Orleans stringer, whose articles *Life* used quite frequently, was famous in New Orleans for seeing a mafioso behind every French Quarter lamppost (that was how he made his living) at a time when everyone else in Louisiana seemed to know that the old, alleged mafia had already "gone legitimate." Perhaps it was David Chandler, then, who saw a glorified gofer as a key assistant and confidant. In an example of incredibly careless, even incompetent journalism, *Life* almost certainly used Chandler's facts without attribution or confirmation.

So much for a "little" mistake, unlike such a great company as Time-Life, which had some of the best journalists in the world in 1967, as they do today. Nevertheless, they unwittingly and negatively affected the outcome of a presidential election. *Life* magazine's so-called exposé of a nonexistent connection between McKeithen and the New Orleans mafia almost certainly cost the Democrats their old Solid South and prolonged the Vietnam tragedy, perhaps causing many thousands of American and Vietnamese young men to lose their lives. Miserable, careless journalism . . . with sad consequences to mankind. At least that's what Mary and I believe to this day, and I know that is what John McKeithen believed to his grave. Anyone who would say that Hubert Humphrey's selection of McKeithen as his vice-presidential running mate wouldn't have made any difference against Richard Nixon and his Southern Strategy simply did not know the man Mary Dixon and I knew.

Moreover, there is a really good case for saying that those unfortunate, inaccurate, strange *Life* stories of September 1967 cost McKeithen the presidency of the United States. Hubert Humphrey apparently knew by late 1975 or early 1976 that he was ill with terminal cancer. If a Humphrey-McKeithen ticket had won in 1968 and 1972, an ill Humphrey might have resigned in 1975 or '76, and McKeithen, a superb campaigner and orator, would have been a formidable presidential candidate of his own in 1976.

McKeithen would have been a wonderful president. He was a good, decent man and smart as hell. The entire world would have been so much better off, and American families would have been spared the heartbreak that so many had to bear because of failed, disgraceful leadership. There would have been no Pres. Richard Nixon, the one person in America most responsible for the dreadful acrimony today between our two national political parties. However, the first consequence of a McKeithen presidency would have been several national football championships for the LSU Tigers, not many years after Paul Dietzel's 1958 Tigers and long before Nick Saban's great 2003 triumph. I'm kidding, of course. Or maybe I'm not, as John McKeithen was a huge LSU football fan.

No one can question that a McKeithen White House in late 1975 or early 1976, plus a four-year term of his own, would have meant many billions of dollars to Louisiana and an improved educational system for the state. John McKeithen's greatest interest in life, other than his family and politics, was education, for both black and white. He felt it shameful that blacks were often denied education and a chance at a productive life as a result of their skin color. He talked about education every time we visited, on hundreds of occasions, particularly his dream of making Louisiana State University into "one of the world's great educational institutions," as he put it. Indeed, LSU today seems to be on the verge of becoming a truly great, world-class university, but it almost certainly would have achieved that status years ago with a McKeithen presidency.

Finally, bet your last dollar that a President McKeithen would have rebuilt Category 5 levees along that fateful 17th Street Canal. Hurricane Katrina would have been inconsequential for New Orleanians and would already be forgotten.

I know that McKeithen, right or wrong, blamed the "Mafia Misinformation Affair" directly on Henry Luce, publisher of *Life*. I for one do not believe that Henry Luce would have intruded himself into such a situation. Indeed, had this been the case, his editors would have checked very, very carefully the accuracy of those words "key assistant and confidant" — and thrown them in the trash can.

Incidentally, The Editor in New Orleans must have known that Aubrey Young was nothing close to how *Life* had described him in print. Almost nothing was more disgraceful than to allow *Life* magazine to get away with a hatchet job — even if unintentionally — on a great Louisianian. The Editor blew it again. A staunch defense of this truly great governor by the *New Orleans Times-Picayune* would have generated many days of superb news stories. To this day the *Times-Picayune* should be embarrassed to have allowed *Life* magazine to run roughshod over our governor. A well-conceived, carefully documented series of stories and investigations was a Pulitzer Prize available for the taking by the *Times-Picayune.*

My nephew, Julian McPhillips, of Montgomery, Alabama, was the prime motivator behind this book, urging me over several years to put down on paper many of the things I know that are not known or not well known to the public. Julian is one powerful, brilliant, tough lawyer, almost certainly my best friend and confidant beside my wife and sons. Admirable in every respect. Recently, I told Julian of my *Life* magazine discoveries and how angry I am that they would misuse their power so carelessly and in my opinion so negligently. Recounting some of the things I say in this book I inquired of him, "Have I libeled those people in any way?" His answer was, in effect, "Hell, no. I think they exposed themselves with what they did. I'd love to sue *them.*"

A good friend, now deceased, who knew of Aubrey Young accompanied me on one of my earlier visits to Loyola University's superb Monroe Library, eventually asking, "Oh, just out of curiosity, can you show me *Life*'s four little words, 'key assistant and confidant'?" On Monroe's third floor I pulled out the bound volume of *Life* 1967 issues, turned to September 29, 1967, located those four words and pointed to them. My friend leaned over, adjusted his glasses, looked where I was pointing, paused momentarily and said, "Oh, yes, you've got them, David, nailed to the cross." My friend added, "My God, four little words that changed history, almost certainly for the worse," he sighed. I took one last lingering look.

I had great respect back in the 1960s for the entire Time-Life organization, as I do today. They publish some of the best magazines in the world. Regardless, Time-Life owes the family of John McKeithen an apology. Even today, forty years late, it would be nice.

Time-Life did great harm to our state and to a great man and, as it turned out, to our country. I give the publication the benefit of the doubt, allowing that it made an honest mistake by relying on a New Orleans stringer. Even so, it did not use its own in-house people for such an important series of articles. No one in history, no one who ever knew Aubrey Young, has agreed with *Life*'s description of him. I challenge anyone, even today, to find just one person in the entire state of Louisiana who would be willing to describe Aubrey Young as anything remotely close to being "a key assistant and confidant" of our late governor John J. McKeithen.

I do believe it was a coincidence that *Life* printed such an incredibly inaccurate article in 1967 associating Gov. John McKeithen of Louisiana by innuendo with the New Orleans mafia just as he and Hubert Humphrey were becoming good friends and political allies. And I do think it was a coincidence that *Time*, owned by *Life*'s parent company, seemingly leaned toward Richard Nixon in 1968 and once again four years later. Nevertheless, the articles created a tragic setback for Louisiana, and for America. How could one say otherwise after Watergate, Vietnam, Spiro Agnew's imprisonment on petty criminal charges, and Richard Nixon's resignation under impeachment circumstances for organizing a criminal break-in of Democratic headquarters in the Watergate Hotel in D.C.?

Is all of this far fetched? Mary and I didn't think so then, and we don't think so now. In a sense all of this was a tragedy for the United States of America. A monumental, fascinating scandal that changed America forever.

CHAPTER X

Political Wisdoms

In 1972, John McKeithen, for all intents and purposes, left political life when his second term as governor expired. At that time, if I had had all my wits about me, I would have found a way to convince John Mecom, Jr., owner of the New Orleans Saint, to appoint John McKeithen as his president and general manager. Now that would have been interesting!

Am I kidding? No, but perhaps not a good thing. An NFL squad composed entirely of ex-LSU players might not have been the best thing for our Saints. Here, I am kidding, of course. McKeithen knew football fairly well. He was a truly brilliant man, a born great leader, who would have found a way to win by hiring the right personnel. Great leaders win, which is what pro football is all about.

I think he would have taken the job. John McKeithen was not a wealthy man. In those days a top president-general manager of an NFL club would have drawn a salary of $250,000 to $500,000. Today, a first-rate GM would range $2 million and up. With McKeithen in that spot, all the bad coaches that Mecom hired between 1972 and 1984, usually on a whim, would never have been hired. And we would have been spared years of frustrations with the Saints. Why? Because John McKeithen was a winner. Never think otherwise. Even his few critics would agree. One lesson that McKeithen taught me was the political power of football, a power that in the past I have put to use to help our state and our city.

Goodbye LSU Tigers or Goodbye David Duke

Around 1991, I became involved in still another Louisiana

political campaign. I was sitting in our family's antiques and paintings gallery worrying about a possible David Duke governorship. A Duke election would do mortal harm to Louisiana, including our family business, which was so dependent upon visitors and major conventions. No convention manager would want to come to a state where there would have been endless protest picketing outside our mammoth convention halls, no matter how delightful New Orleans might be. New industry would definitely be turned off.

I was desperate to find something to beat David Duke, who wore a Nazi uniform while a student at LSU, constantly preached messages of hate against Jews, blacks, Apaches, Eskimos, Martians, and anyone else. What a joke! Yet, somehow, he sounded convincing to many people, actually leading former governor Edwin Edwards in polls by a slight 1 percent, according to Edwards himself, as they entered a runoff in 1991.

I had paid for a few local commercials with a message along these lines: "David Duke's supporters claim that Duke as governor would not hurt our convention and tourism business. They're absolutely right. David Duke wouldn't hurt our convention business, he would kill it." But Duke remained a serious threat, still slightly ahead in polls.

At that point, thank goodness, an idea jumped into my mind. My winning idea was simply to point out the adverse effect that a Duke victory would have on football recruiting by the LSU Tigers, a team for which top young African-American athletes always are in high demand. Immediately, I felt that David Duke would be defeated, probably easily, that the choice between our LSU Tigers and David Duke was a no-brainer. I started laughing so hard that my two oldest sons, Frank and Shea, who knew that I was alone and not on the telephone, came rushing into my office fearing that old Dad had finally flipped out (what they did not know was that I had flipped out years earlier). I stated immediately, "The election is over. I'm going to run a commercial myself [I still had a little notoriety left from Superdome and Saints days] that I guarantee will win the election for Edwards. Duke is through." As soon as I read my winning commercial, both sons roared, saying immediately, "You're right, Dad. It's over."

Out of my own pocket, I paid for the following message, booked via our ad agency, at half a dozen north and central Louisiana TV stations, markets where Edwards needed help the most: "I'm Dave Dixon. I want to tell it to you just the way it is. It's goodbye LSU Tigers or it's goodbye David Duke. Take your choice. If David Duke is sitting in the Governor's Mansion, how can we recruit the best football talent in America to come to LSU? Take your choice: LSU Tigers or David Duke."

Thirty days later Edwin Edwards came into our office on Royal Street to show me a Mason-Dixon poll. "Here I am thirty days ago, actually a little bit behind this clown. Today we're 250,000 votes to the good, and we're going to win by 350,000 votes on Election Day." He actually won by 384,000 after trailing at the beginning of the runoff. "You know what all of this tells me?" he questioned. Dutifully I asked, "What?" Edwards continued, "This tells me that 250,000 Bubbas, Rednecks, and ex-Ku Kluxers have suddenly decided that they like LSU football a whole lot more than they dislike blacks. Do you have any more ideas?" We laughed together.

I went on to tell him that I had known that the LSU Athletic Department could not participate in politics in any form but that I had run the proposed commercial by Joe Dean, LSU's director of athletics, as a courtesy. If there had been anything in the commercial to which he seriously objected, I simply would not run it. Joe Dean's reply was that I should run it. He believed it was an election winner. He explained, "I have twenty-eight coaches here ready to jump out of windows. Right now it would be extremely difficult to recruit top black kids."

Edwards and I became friends during all the David Duke nonsense. In most respects he was a very good man who did a lot of good things for a lot of poor people. "Football," Edwin once said to me in one of his philosophical moods, "will help bring the races together." Didn't John McKeithen say almost the same thing?

A Sports Lottery to Benefit Education

America's greatest opportunity today for improvement in our daily lives clearly rests in education. Education is the cure-all for most of society's social, racial, and economic ills, worldwide, an idea that has been with me since I was a young boy and my parents questioned why governments couldn't educate the entire population, especially the poor, so that all citizens would be better off. Their question was repeated to me almost verbatim in 1966 by John McKeithen.

There is a desperate need all across our society for sharply upgraded state school systems with strict local administration funded by the states but ideally supported with strong federal financial assistance. Such improvements can be funded significantly, it would seem, by a well-designed sports lottery involving picking winners of NFL, NBA, or MLB games plus PGA events, all professional, no college games, fifty-two weeks per year. There would be huge interest. Such a lottery would provoke protests from professional leagues screaming about the "integrity" of their particular sport, but I also recognized instantly the incredible potential of such a lottery. Americans love sports, particularly football. Besides, any well-designed sports lottery automatically will be "fix-proof." With odds well into the millions, how can anyone fix a statistical two- or three-million-to-one shot? It would take hundreds of thousands of such fixes! Initial protests from the NFL, NBA, MLB, and PGA will be substantial, a reflex rather than fact-based. Such protests eventually will be forgotten as realization sinks in that a sports lottery will be fix-proof. Most of all, protests will be forgotten as the leagues begin to realize that a sports lottery inevitably will result in substantial increases in levels of interest in their respective sports, leading to greater fan attendance and TV ratings. Eventually colleges will understand that fact and request inclusion, too.

Any state-sponsored sports lottery should be dedicated to a cause that would have strong popular appeal. Ideally such a cause would be grade-school education, particularly for the poor, such as inner-city and rural children. Our country does not have a bigger, sadder problem than the terrible conditions that exist in inner-city schools almost everywhere and in poor rural areas. But not only grade-school students or the poor should be beneficiaries. Education for everyone, preschools, grade schools, high schools, colleges, and universities, would receive revenues by the sports lottery idea that follows.

Before a state legislature would be willing to dedicate revenues from a sports lottery specifically to education rather than to the general fund, it would want to know whether a sports lottery would create shortfalls of revenue from existing lotteries. The flip side of that coin is that educators would be concerned that legislatures would decrease present levels of funding for education once the revenues from a sports lottery would come rolling in. Both possibilities could be adequately protected quite simply within the legislative act creating the sports lottery, requiring the lottery to reimburse such shortfalls on a reasonable basis.

There are sufficient weekly sports events in America to form a modified daily sports lottery, much as with today's numbers lotteries. The concept and rules behind the sports lottery can be easily summarized in four steps.

1. Players pick the winners of eight games per week from the NFL, NBA, MLB, or combinations thereof, or from weekly PGA golf with focus on "majors" such as the Masters, the U.S. Open, the British Open, and the PGA championship. No college games in any sport would be included.

2. All games would be equalized with point spreads, always expressed in fractions so that ties would be eliminated. Thus, a 3-point favorite in football or basketball would be stated as $2^1/_2$ points or $3^1/_2$ points. In baseball a one-run favorite would be stated at $1^1/_2$ runs. The normal odds against picking all eight equalized games correctly would be 256 to 1.

3. A statistician-mathematician would be employed to suggest efficient "add-ons" to increase the odds of a blockbuster award from 256 to 1 into the millions to one, whatever would create the equivalent of the incredibly popular Powerball in existing lotteries. For example, a lottery player might be asked to predict the actual scores of, say, three or four games, the winning margin for each of the games, perhaps the total points scored in each game, or any combination of add-ons.

4. These add-ons may seem complicated, but they are not. Any reasonably capable high school student could select efficient

add-ons simply by making an analysis, for example, of actual NFL scores for an entire regular season in football (256 games), then computing the likelihood, or odds, of selecting correctly the margin of victory, total points scored, or the final score of a designated game. The same could be done for baseball, basketball, hockey, or almost any sport, even PGA golf. Whatever the format, there must be simplicity for ease of processing and mass usage. A ballot printed in or distributed by newspapers as paid advertising would be tremendously helpful.

It also would be a simple task to devise a "Quick Pick" ticket so that a sports lottery customer would not have to take the time to make individual choices of winning teams (after point spreads). Computers would simply assign numbers to represent each winning team plus an exact score for each winning game. The likelihood of a computer printing any two cards alike could be in the millions to one, depending upon the number of games listed for that week. The customer would know always his exact selections of winners and scores for each game.

The distribution of proceeds I present here is just as a guess, to be studied further by experts, but I suggest that 50 percent of revenues, after expenses, might go to the state for education, 25 percent might be allocated to weekly prizes, and 25 percent might go to a blockbuster award (whose winner guessed all eight games that week correctly and accurately predicted all "add-ons").

The proceeds from each week that there is no blockbuster winner would be carried over to create an ever-growing purse. If no blockbuster winners emerge, the blockbuster accumulated fund might be awarded every three or six months to the card that is closest to correct, or for whatever stipulated period would create maximum results.

This idea is dedicated to the people of Louisiana. However, these suggestions, particularly the creation of a blockbuster award in the many millions of dollars, should capture the public's imagination and produce revenues nationwide that will be of huge assistance to educators everywhere. A sports lottery and ensuing publicity would focus enormous attention on education itself and ideally improve the lives of children and eventually create a better future for all Americans.

CHAPTER XI

Help from the
Times-Picayune

New Orleans mayor, Victor Hugo Schiro, had appointed The Editor as chairman of the Mayor's Super Bowl Committee in 1969, I believe. Mayor Schiro, who never lost an election, had superb political instincts. His appointment of The Editor was a stroke of genius. The Editor could hardly criticize himself, so all the news, with massive *Times-Picayune* coverage, about New Orleans' attendance at an NFL Super Bowl site selection meeting in Miami was very positive. Mayor Schiro knew, as did I, that the Super Bowl site for 1971 probably had already been determined. It would be in New Orleans, in Tulane University's 83,000-capacity football stadium. That Super Bowl was not ours to win, it was ours not to lose.

For me, one personal incident cast a small shadow on my presence at that NFL meeting. I knew each NFL owner quite well, having attended all NFL and AFL league meetings for six or seven years. When The Editor asked me (to my surprise) to take him around and introduce him to the various owners individually, I was very happy to oblige. In the course of making those introductions, I spotted Ralph Wilson, the influential owner of the Buffalo Bills, a really first-class person, standing alone at a lobby newsstand. I hustled my editor "friend" over to meet Ralph, a former AFL now NFL owner and a particularly good personal friend.

The Editor promptly asked, "Mr. Wilson, what will it take to get the next Super Bowl for our city?" Ralph answered: "Well, first, make sure that you have a strong presentation and in particular a strong presenter, someone like Dave Dixon here. All the owners already know him." I winced, knowing instinctively and immediately, that somewhere, sometime, The Editor would make me pay for that compliment. Shortly thereafter I went back to my hotel room and made my daily update to Governor McKeithen. I covered my ass, to put it bluntly (not that I had to cover anything with McKeithen). I knew that the governor and I had the same opinion of The Editor.

Laughingly, I described the Ralph Wilson encounter, saying, "I will pay one hell of a price for that compliment. Come to think of it, our editor friend will find some reason to call *you*. Our mayor won't do anything more than laugh—privately— after assuring The Editor that he will look into the matter 'promptly.' He'll call you. Watch and see."

Sure enough, one week later McKeithen, roaring with laughter, called to say, "Dave, you predicted it exactly. Man, your friend The Editor really unloaded on you, saying that you had physically interfered with his presentation and on, and on."

Actually, I had not seen the presentation, as my lobbying had been done, and I had departed for home two days earlier. I could plead "not guilty" quite legitimately, as it was physically impossible for me to interfere with a Miami presentation while in New Orleans. The Editor lost another one, this time without any real effort on my part.

But, let me give the devil his due. The Editor had arranged to have Al Hirt as a surprise entertainer at the big NFL dinner party. From all accounts Al, who brought along Hoagy Carmichael, was a smash hit and helped to solidify future Super Bowls for our great city, even though the Super Bowl site of the moment apparently had been chosen well before the NFL meeting. The decision had been made when the NFL resolved to award their big game on something of a rotation basis. Even so, The Editor did a great job, as did Al Hirt. Predictably, NFL owners fell in love with our city, as it became the site of many Super Bowls in the immediate years ahead. I give The Editor enormous credit for a job well done.

"Promoter" Dave Dixon

Though the *Times-Picayune* had warmed toward the Saints, by then our editor friend decided it was time to put me in my place.

He gave orders to his staff to refer to me as a "promoter," a reference that endured at the *Picayune* well past The Editor's inevitable departure. The continued reference surprised me a bit. I knew, of course, that The Editor had used this "promoter" description contemptuously. I guess his objective was to make me look a bit like the fight promoter, Don King, the guy with the wild hair that sticks straight up in the front. Well, Editor, you lost again. I don't have enough hair to "stick up" anywhere—not for the past fifty years. Or maybe The Editor wanted to link me in the public's mind with "Leaping Louie" Messina, a somewhat notorious local fight promoter of the 1950s.

My wife, Mary Dixon, got tired of the continued, insulting reference a few years ago and finally wrote Ashton Phelps, Jr., the *Times-Picayune*'s publisher, very diplomatically asking him to please cease referring to me as a promoter. Ashton, a gentleman, responded with a nice note and a telephone call of apology and a statement of unawareness. Mary was and is well satisfied.

The "old" *Picayune* had cause to be miffed at me and at all those who worked so hard to bring the New Orleans Saints to the city. We got the NFL franchise for our city and built a magnificent Superdome, while the *Picayune* never lifted a finger editorially to help. Even without the potentially powerful backing of the city's dominant paper, we—and the people of New Orleans—won every battle decisively.

Before his death, I consulted the great Buddy Diliberto, a close friend and a person very knowledgeable of The Editor's attitude and actions during the 1960s and 1970s. To my knowledge no private citizen ever has taken on the "old" *Times-Picayune* as I have done herein. I asked Buddy whether I am being politically and diplomatically unwise to take on the *Picayune* and The Editor, even if so many years later. My friend's reply: "Not if you want your book to be honest!"

As I was writing these pages in 2005, I received even more emphatic support for publicizing past difficulties with the *Picayune*. I encountered my dear friend of seventy-two years, Robert M. "Bobby" Monsted, a highly respected founding partner of our New Orleans Pro Football Club, Inc., the vehicle that we used to make our franchise and Superdome efforts. Bobby passed away only weeks after reading the initial manuscript of this book, which I had hand delivered to him. I told him of my frustration with The Editor, stating that I hoped that I had not been too rough in this book on either The Editor or the *Picayune.* Bobby laughed and replied, "How could you have been too rough? Those guys never lifted a finger to help us. Not once, from 1960 through All Saints Day 1966. They're okay today, but they were terrible then. They nitpicked the Superdome almost to death. Too rough? Nah!"

As confirmation of what I have stated, note that Jack Tims did not ask his *Times-Picayune* editor to interview the members of the Superdome's advisory committee when I "covertly" approached him in his office that day in 1967. Instead, he gave that crucial assignment to Walter Cowan of the *New Orleans States,* the *Picayune*'s afternoon counterpart at that time.

Mary reminds me that the first editorially positive words from the *Times-Picayune* about the New Orleans Saints occurred significantly on All Saints Day, November 1, 1966, when the franchise was finally and definitely awarded to our city. The *Picayune* admitted that it was a nice day for New Orleans. By comparison, the *New Orleans States* published a huge black headline, "N.O. GOES PRO!", a takeoff on our "Let's Go Pro" ad campaign. Mary also reminds me that the first admission from yesteryear's *Times-Picayune* that the Superdome might not be detrimental to the city occurred about one month after that magnificent building was opened. This bit of information was communicated in one small, grudging editorial paragraph.

The paper's traditional excuse for lack of civic support is that they cannot be expected to be cheerleaders. Why the hell not? Today's *Picayune* is an enthusiastic cheerleader for anything that is worthwhile, and if ever there were a project that the *Picayune* should have cheered on, it was the NFL/Superdome project.

Still, yesteryear's *Picayune* had a number of top people, especially my friends Iris Kelso and Paul Atkinson, very honest, very factual, who covered the Superdome on virtually an everyday basis. However, The Editor kept them subjugated, at least to a degree, whether they knew it or not.

Dave Dixon receives *Times-Picayune* Loving Cup from publisher
Ashton Phelps, 1989. (© 2007 The Times-Picayune Publishing Co. All
rights reserved. Used with permission of The Times-Picayune.)

The following story typifies The Editor as he was so many years ago, when he made my every day challenging but fun and exciting. Mary says that I enjoy combat. In 1971, I became increasingly alarmed before Superdome construction bidding that costs seemed to be rising. To reduce the costs, we took a good hard look at elevators and escalators, among other things. Finally, Buster Curtis, our magnificent architect, agreed that we could eliminate from the plans one elevator and, I believe, one escalator, plus a few extra seats. Our opponent, The Editor, ever looking for some kind of misdeed, must have sensed foul play and he sent one of his top reporters to find out about that "missing" elevator. His reporter telephoned our home in the evening to talk to me. I was working late, so he talked to Mary, asking her in effect what happened to the "missing" elevator and those eliminated seats.

As he persisted, Mary finally said, "Well, I remember now. David had the men bring that elevator out here to our home. It's in our backyard along with the extra seats. Alongside the invisible escalator." I think she, too, enjoyed a little combat. Not with me, of course; I was a pussycat for that gal. At any rate, The Editor was outmatched again, this time by Mary Dixon.

While his attempts to block our franchise and Superdome efforts were very trying, I really have only minimal lingering bitterness toward The Editor, who lost every single battle he instituted against us over a period of many years. Though an accomplished, talented progress blocker, at his best The Editor was a good newsman, and I have great respect for his fine family and friends.

The *Picayune* was an entity that I felt was a possible opponent every day of my life during those years, but today it is a paper for which I have genuine respect, and they know it. Today's *Picayune* is an excellent newspaper, with full credit belonging to publisher Ashton Phelps, Jr., and editor Jim Amoss, along with his predecessor, Charles Ferguson. Today the paper boasts an extremely impressive executive staff, top to bottom, and terrific reporters. Sure enough, the *New Orleans Times-Picayune* won richly deserved Pulitzer Prizes for their post-Katrina performance. Under extremely difficult, almost primitive working conditions, they displayed journalism at its very best.

CHAPTER XII

Opening the Dome

I remember once walking down Gravier Street, probably in late 1962, and hearing a passerby tell his friend, "That's Dave Dixon, the nut who says that New Orleans will average 50,000 in attendance and sell 20,000 season tickets for a pro team." Well, we sold 37,000 season tickets in our first franchise year, 1967, and averaged nearly 70,000 attendance, tops in the NFL, with a rather pitiful but beloved expansion team. New Orleans is a helluva football town, always has been. This was the NFL of 1967, and those figures were just about the best in the league for just about the league's worst team, far better than Atlanta's first-year 1966 figures.

Usually the New Orleans Saints sell about 53,000 season tickets today and sell out every game in our 68,000-capacity Louisiana Superdome despite only one playoff game victory prior to 2006. That is thirty-nine years of existence and only one playoff victory until our 2006 season with Sean Payton, Drew Brees, and Reggie Bush. The city responded, and 2007 saw a season ticket sellout of every seat in our Louisiana Superdome. So much for the naysayers, I feel pretty good about how things turned out for our wonderful city.

A Superdome Seating Fiasco

Before the Superdome opened, there were a few roadblocks in planning that needed to be overcome. I had left the Superdome Commission to return to private business when John McKeithen's term of office expired in early 1972 and Edwin

Dixon family's Superdome Christmas card, 1970.

Edwards' term began. However, I did remain somewhat informed on key construction matters by Buster Curtis and by the Superdome staff engineer, Mark Carrigan. I felt I had to act when I discovered that with the Superdome's completion during the summer of 1975, the New Orleans Saints and the Superdome Commission made a dreadful, even if accidental, mistake.

There are two basic Superdome seating configurations. One is primarily for baseball, with the Plaza Level sideline movable stands pushed back approximately twenty-five feet for the additional room needed for a good baseball layout. Such a move creates an open area in each of the Plaza Level's four corners. Four additional sections of stands, each seating about 750, creating approximately 3,000 extra seats, can be moved into these four areas. This is the configuration that is used today only for Sugar Bowls and Super Bowls in order to increase seating capacity from approximately 68,500 to roughly 71,500. This configuration does not make it impossible or difficult for sideline Plaza patrons to see, but the view is not nearly as good as in the regular season configuration.

It was never the intention of the Superdome Commission, of which John McKeithen and I were a part, to use the baseball configuration for regular season Saints or Tulane football simply because all sight lines for Plaza sideline seats are adversely impacted, being approximately twenty-five feet farther from the playing field. Frankly, to use the baseball configuration for football would be terribly unfair to regular season football patrons, nearly 100 percent of whom are tax-paying residents of New Orleans and nearby parishes.

Therefore, I was horrified when I realized from newspaper and TV accounts that the Saints were using the baseball configuration, with its 3,000 extra seats, to sell football tickets, and Superdome officials were allowing them to do so. I immediately assumed that because initial publicity regarding the completed Superdome was so favorable, the Saints organization figured that it could sell out the Superdome using the larger configuration with 3,000 extra seats tucked into the four Superdome baseball corners. I initially thought this decision was based on greed, a terrible PR blunder.

However, I had not taken into consideration the fact that on-the-spot Superdome officials such as Edwin Edwards and his stadium commission appointees, plus Mayor Landrieu, Ben Levy, and Bill Connick, were not strong football fans. They would fail to recognize immediately the sight-line concerns so important to the serious, dedicated football fans who would be occupying those expensive Plaza Section sideline seats. Nor would Dick Gordon, the Saints general manager, the former astronaut. Though good people and good friends of mine, they were not football oriented. I ultimately reached the conclusion that this entire situation had developed out of a rather incredible error by the Superdome Commission and by the New Orleans Saints, but not by greed.

The next day, I attended a periodic Superdome Commission meeting, jam-packed to my surprise with hundreds of invitees and fans. After asking to speak, I told them of my disappointment as a fan that they were allowing the Saints to use the baseball configuration. I pointed out that this was a serious mistake, affecting viewing quality for thousands of fans in the lower sideline Plaza Sections. I suggested that they correct this mistake immediately. Right away I realized that neither the Saints nor the Superdome officials were willing to change to the intended, correct configuration with far better viewing for spectators. I could not believe what was happening. I proceeded to file a lawsuit that same day, asking that the Saints and the Stadium Commission be required to use the correct seating plan; otherwise, thousands of fans would be denied the quality of seating to which they were entitled. I was very uncomfortable with the huge publicity that erupted.

A few days later the Saints and the Superdome Commission asked me whether I would drop the lawsuit if the Saints promised to use the proper configuration in the future, after that first season. They recognized that our position was correct, but insisted that it would be a logistical nightmare to reassign the thousands of seat sales that already had been made. I knew that no such logistical nightmare existed, simply because few seats, if any, had been sold in those remote extra corner sections, but instinct told me that a little face-saving was probably the wiser course. Besides, I believed then that the mistake was not greed but misjudgment. I agreed to drop the lawsuit.

Sure enough, I learned a few days later that the Saints had not persuaded Superdome officials to allow them to use the larger capacity baseball configuration. Both sides, I realized, simply did not know any better. Rather incredible but true!

I wished by then, several days later, that I had been smart enough to figure out a way to make this correction privately. Immediate action was called for, but I should have handled the situation more diplomatically. I am embarrassed, and I apologize to Dick Gordon.

A Great Irony

I have felt from the beginning of today's stadium controversy over whether or not the Saints need a new or revitalized arena that the sensible thing would be, ironically, to move the Plaza Level sideline stands closer to the field, rather than backward as in 1975. Several rows of choice sideline seats or suites could be added at the tops of both Westside Plaza and Eastside Plaza stands in the space created by the forward movement. Concourse entertainment areas could be added behind these new seats all the way to existing concourses. The West Side press box should be relocated from its present Loge position to the top of the Terrace section.

I believe that this modified view of our 2005 Superdome could be the Saints' position as a sensible standby for at least the next twenty years. However, under no circumstances should the state commit to building a new stadium at any fixed future date, such as 2020 or 2025. Who's to know what will be the circumstances at a specific future date?

Almost certainly there will be three schools of thought regarding Superdome renovations: plans A, B, or C. Plan A would be a relatively low-cost revamping, as roughly described in preceding paragraphs, not to exceed $60 million. Plan B, at a cost of $160 million or more, probably will be introduced by Superdome Management Group (SMG). Theoretically, Plan B will produce close to 100 percent of the increased revenue streams now being realized at the new stadiums built in recent years in competing NFL cities, thus substantially reducing the need for the small market subsidy now being paid to the Saints by the state. This plan would be strongly endorsed by Doug Thornton, the highly capable chief executive of SMG locally, as good a person as I have encountered anywhere. Plan C would be the Saints' own proposal, rumored to be Plan A plus an imaginative development of the surrounding area owned by the state of Louisiana. Almost certainly Tom Benson will want to retain the current small market subsidy, no matter the plan chosen.

One thing is certain. An extremely interesting public discussion will follow. I can see merit to both sides. Today I favor Plan A. Tomorrow it could be B or C or some combination thereof. My prediction? It will be Plan B, not a bad choice if a really top architect is selected. Extreme care should be taken to prevent anything that will change the Superdome's exterior appearance, such as cutting holes to admit light and views of the city. Buster Curtis was a genius, don't mess with his "look."

The Saints at the Superdome

Time seemed to race by between the NFL 1967 opener for our New Orleans Saints at venerable old Tulane Stadium and the first regular season game in the Superdome. Maybe the time seemed so short because I was consumed with projects or because there was little to admire about team's many losing seasons, but at least they were our losing team. But now America's most magnificent stadium, the Louisiana Superdome, awaited our New Orleans Saints.

Completed, the stadium was ready to be dedicated by August 1975. On August 3, at 2:00 P.M., the culmination of a dream for Mary and me and our three sons, Frank, Shea, and Stuart, after thousands of hours of work, planning, thinking, some extra maneuvering, even a bit of scheming here and there, and we were ready to dedicate our spectacular Louisiana Superdome, designed magnificently and superbly by the man I knew was a

Dave Dixon and Governor McKeithen opening bids for contractors, 1971.

genius of an architect, New Orleans' own Buster Curtis. For our Superdome he was the best architect in the world, and he proved it.

Except for a bit of touching up and polishing here and there, our Louisiana Superdome was ready for our political leaders, namely Gov. Edwin Edwards and New Orleans mayor Moon Landrieu, to dedicate it to the people of our city and state. Beyond even my expectations, the building was even greater and more breathtaking in its way than was Huey Long's Louisiana Capitol Building, built in Baton Rouge in the late 1920s.

you're invited to the largest open house ever held!

(it's free!)

On August 3rd, in the heart of downtown New Orleans, the world's greatest building will be dedicated. Your Louisiana Superdome.

You're invited to this special occasion. A day dedicated to the people of Louisiana who built this magnificent structure — the largest enclosed stadium-arena-convention facility in the world.

Bring your family and friends to share in the historic celebration. The dedication of the Louisiana Superdome.

Dedication - August 3rd

Program — Noon to 8 p.m.
Dedication ceremonies — 2 p.m.

Entertainment by
Al Hirt, Pete Fountain,
and many others.

**Grand Opening Ceremonies -
Aug. 29th to Sept. 14th**

Louisiana Superdome

Superdome dedication program, August 3, 1975.

John McKeithen was retired, back home in Columbia, Louisiana, and Edwin Edwards was governor. He gave tremendous and eloquent recognition and credit to John McKeithen, Louisiana's best governor ever in my book. Edwin even threw a few accolades my way and to a richly deserving Mayor Moon Landrieu.

From that splendid dedication ceremony on August 3, 1975, to the first real game (I hate "preseason" games) with the Cincinnati Bengals before a packed house at the Superdome on September 28, 1975, the team and the Superdome received great, great praise everywhere. The Saints played their first regular season game in front of a sellout crowd of proud New Orleanians (myself a New Orleanian to my toenails). Guess who won? The Bengals, of course, 21-0, but that was John Mecom's Saints.

I have written about the most memorable football moments in our city's history. It embarrasses me, as a man, that I weep easily, and I can remember at least three football instances that made me choke up a bit. The first occurred a few weeks before the August 1963 preseason NFL doubleheader at Tulane Stadium, a dozen or more years before our Superdome came into being, when a black gentleman expressed such joy at being able to purchase tickets to the game on an equal basis. The second moment was at the first Saints game ever, at home, at New Orleans, at wonderful old Tulane Stadium. The opening of the 1975 regular season football game in the Superdome was the third moment. I was so proud of my great friend, architect Nathaniel C. "Buster" Curtis, Jr., that when I absorbed our Superdome's first football moment that, yes, I know that I shed a tear or two.

CHAPTER XIII

Conversion

Quitting Smoking

My quest to secure the Saints and the Superdome for our city has infiltrated every aspect of my life, leading to a change of heart concerning several things, even my addiction to cigarettes. As I stated earlier, my father was a heavy smoker, more cigars than cigarettes. I was already an occasional smoker at age fifteen, but cigarettes looked so harmless, so tiny, that I always felt that I could quit smoking whenever I wanted. I used that lamest of excuses from the beginning. Unfortunately, it wasn't until years later that I made the decision to quit. By then, of course, I was so addicted that it was difficult — agonizingly difficult — to do. I empathize with anyone who has an addiction, whether alcohol, cigarettes, food, or drugs.

I believe that I became a heavy smoker in the Marine Corps (seven cents per pack at the PX), but it wasn't until 1963 that I really wanted to quit. I was calling on NFL owners and officials, and I felt that I had to quit to make good impressions for an expansion franchise for our city and to make sure that we got our Superdome built. If I had not quit smoking from 1963 through 1969 there probably would have been no New Orleans Saints, no Louisiana Superdome. In addition, I was forty, nearing my father's age of forty-five when he died of cancer, caused by smoking. Most of all, I had three fine young sons, then ages thirteen, eleven, and eight, and I did not want to inflict the smoking habit on them at their most impressionable age. To this day, none of my sons has ever smoked, nor do they have problems with alcohol. One day in June, I decided that I had smoked my last cigarette.

I really believed that I had quit for life on that June day in 1963. But Havana cigars, boycotted during the most contentious part of Fidel Castro's regime, were beginning to creep back into circulation by 1969. A good friend offered me a five-dollar Havana cigar, equivalent to a thirty-dollar cigar today, while celebrating some little Superdome milestone or victory. I lit up, enjoyed it immensely, and eventually went home and went to bed.

Driving to the Superdome area the next day, I wanted a smoke so badly that I left the expressway to buy a pack of cigarettes, figuring I'd only smoke that morning and then go back to abstinence later in the day. Baloney, that kind of rationale meant that I was hooked again, or perhaps still. One puff is as lethal for a reformed smoker as one little sip of beer is for a recovering alcoholic. I am living testimony. I was smoking again.

In late 1971, I received a telephone call from Jimmy Coleman, a family friend and great civic leader, who for many years had been the lawyer for my stepfather's late business partner, Tom Dutton. Jimmy told me that he was concerned about their Lincoln-Mercury automobile dealership. Sales had fallen badly after the death of both principals, and he was asking me to take a major role in the dealership in an effort to rebuild sales and profits.

I did not want to remain for too long, as I did not feel that running an automobile dealership was what I wanted to do for the rest of my life, but the timing was good. I felt that the major parts of the Saints-Superdome struggle were completed and behind us, and I was ready for a new challenge. I accepted Mr. Coleman's offer with a degree of enthusiasm, particularly as it reunited me with my stepbrother, Louis Clay, Jr., called "Sonny" within the family. My arrival at the Clay-Dutton dealership seemed to reinvigorate Sonny, a likable person. His father had been a well-intentioned but tough taskmaster, perhaps dwelling a bit too much on negatives rather than positives, an observation I would pass along to any young father today. Accentuate the positive.

I was pleased to see that Sonny and I were going to be a good team. Sales picked up, morale picked up, and things generally went well at a reinvigorated Clay-Dutton Lincoln-Mercury. I enjoyed my brief sojourn in the automobile business, but I knew fairly early that my instinct was correct, this was not what I wanted to do for the rest of my life.

By then I was smoking heavier than ever, with blockbuster headaches occurring every day around 4:00 P.M. I knew it was the cigarettes and the pressures of business that were giving me these terrible headaches. After all, I had had zero headaches — none — during six years (1963-69) of non-smoking, years during which I was always under pressure.

So, again I was desperate to quit. Fortunately, a moment of inspiration arrived. Driving to work one day, I heard one of our usual radio commercials, a "better deals, better service, better everything" type ad, typical of the automobile industry to this day. Suddenly, I wondered whether it would be possible to do a commercial myself, in which I stated that I had quit smoking, in effect putting myself on such a tremendous spot that I would have to permanently quit or leave town in disgrace. Obviously, this commercial would be completely different than anything our competitors were doing, but would it sell cars?

As my mind raced on this new topic, I remembered a Korean importer friend for whom I had recently done a considerable favor. He had told me that he would always sell to me at cost anything I might want from his huge warehouse of imported items. For example, he had once given me a handsome set of stainless steel dinnerware, knives, forks, spoons, etc., selling in department stores for $125.00, telling me that his actual cost was something like $12.00 per set.

I constructed an ad very roughly as follows, knowing that my notoriety from the Saints and the Superdome would make me recognizable to the public: "I'm Dave Dixon. I've quit smoking and I feel so good that I want to make a unique offer to every smoker for miles around. Visit our dealership, Clay-Dutton Lincoln-Mercury at 1515 Poydras, buy any kind of car from us, even a $100 used car, use our great service department, or simply visit our show room, and sign a pledge that you will not smoke for ten days. Come back after those ten days and receive free of charge a beautiful $125.00 set of stainless steel dinnerware. Even non-smokers are eligible. I'm Dave Dixon, I've quit smoking, and I feel wonderful. Honor system prevails." The commercial was worded much better than stated here, and our sales simply exploded. I've never had so much fun in my life.

Guys on the street were stopping me, saying things like, "You're Dave Dixon, aren't you? You so-and-so, my wife jumped all over me, saying, 'If Dave Dixon can quit smoking, why can't you? Go get me that nice gift.'" That was thirty-five years ago, and I have not taken one puff since. Further, I have not had a single headache during those thirty-five years. Not one.

One day, sitting at my desk basking in this great sales surge, I received a telephone call from someone who authoritatively identified himself as an officer of the American Tobacco Institute. He told me that they were going to make an official complaint to Mr. Ford demanding that our franchise be revoked if we did not cease our anti-smoking advertising immediately. I couldn't believe my ears.

There was no way I was going to cancel the ads, not with our sales going through the roof, but being a rookie in the car business, I decided to sort of placate this gentleman, ending our conversation with a few kind words. As my phone hit the receiver, I realized too late that I had just blown one of the great sales opportunities of all time. What I should have done of course was to tell this gentleman that we wanted to cooperate and get his name, title, and telephone number, call back in a couple of days to confirm authenticity, then call a gigantic news conference to state that I was filing suit against these terrible people, who were threatening me personally. With that kind of national publicity and notoriety I would have sold more cars than any dealer almost anywhere. I blew that opportunity, but I haven't smoked since. I intend to reach one hundred, but I would not be here today without those crazy commercials. Actually, I would have found some other way to quit. Cigarettes really were killing me, just as they killed my wonderful father. I hope that any smoker reading these pages will quit immediately. Listen, I'm a weak sister, and I made it. Like that guy who stopped me on the street so many years ago, whose wife told him, "If Dave Dixon can quit smoking, why can't you?"

The Whistle-Blower

A few years ago I had an experience with a courageous woman that left me counting my blessings that I had quit smoking forever around 1971. I know now that Big Tobacco has conspired for many years to make cigarettes more and more addictive, even though they know that lung cancer and other forms of cancer and heart disease will surely follow and cut short the lives of millions of people. If that isn't premeditated murder, what the hell is?

The great whistle-blower of the tobacco industry, believe it or not, is a native New Orleanian. This lady, this whistle-blower, called me one Saturday morning a few years ago at our family's antiques and paintings gallery on Royal Street, now closed. She described some very nice antique furniture pieces that she wanted to sell. I knew from her descriptions that her things almost certainly were authentic eighteenth century, so I went over to her French Quarter residence to see for myself. Sure enough, her furnishings were very nice period pieces. After a few minutes of pleasant negotiations, I bought a number of items from her.

Then, relaxed, she asked if I would like a cup of coffee. I accepted and sat down for a social visit. Almost immediately, she asked, "You don't know who I am, do you?" I replied, "I'm not sure. Tell me." She said, "I'm the whistle-blower of the tobacco industry. I testified before Congress a few days ago. Now I'm in the FBI witness protection program. Standing at the window of the house across the street, you will see two men watching this place. I told them you were coming, which is why no one stopped you when you came to my front door. They're FBI."

I was very uncomfortable to say the least, thinking to myself, "Get the hell out of here as soon as you can, stupid." With billions at stake, even so-called aristocrats will kill. But I was fascinated with what she was telling me. She continued her story: "My husband, a medical doctor, retired a couple of years ago as president of *Philip Morris Research* at company headquarters in Richmond. He brought home a trunk full of research documents, but I had no idea what was really in that trunk.

"One day I spent hours looking for the deed to our house. My husband was out of town so I decided to look in that trunk, thinking that he might have placed the deed there for safe-keeping. I didn't find the deed. Instead I found all these very incriminating documents, including several that indicated that company research was conducted to determine whether a non-carcinogenic cigarette was possible. His conclusion after months of research: Impossible. I also found countless other similarly incriminating documents, such as an assignment to increase addictiveness so that quitting smoking would be very, very difficult. 'Mission accomplished' was my husband's report." she said.

My new friend went on, "He was to testify before a congressional committee. After seeing the content of that trunk, I told him that if he lied before that committee, I would divorce him, that Big Tobacco was no better than a bunch of thugs and murderers. He lied to the committee, and I divorced him. I am ostracized everywhere in Richmond, so I've come back to my birthplace." She was in tears, and I felt very sorry for her.

Shortly thereafter I left her French Quarter home, glanced at the window where the two FBI agents were standing, waved to them, and returned to our gallery. I was uneasy, apprehensive that I had seen photocopies of highly incriminating research documents containing some very plain language. Two nights later Mary and I watched to our amazement this brave lady being interviewed on ABC by Ted Koppel, saying exactly what she had told me in her home. Why is it my luck to stumble so consistently into situations of that type? Where was The Editor when I really needed him?

Heart Surgery and the Church

My decision to quit smoking saved my life, but another conversion, a spiritual one, has shaped my life ever since. As described earlier, during late 1967 and early 1968 I had taken what amounted to a leave of absence from the Superdome to become Lamar Hunt's partner in putting together World Championship Tennis. During my absence, the Superdome

Commission hired a very capable young man named Billy Connick, who knew politics like the back of his hand and enjoyed such activities immensely. Billy, who has become very close to being my closest friend, was and is a devout Catholic, much as is my wife, Mary. I was an Episcopalian who frequently attended Catholic Mass with Mary and our three sons.

During the late spring of 1979 I had just about reached the decision to join the Catholic Church, something that I had been considering for a number of years. However, before taking the final step, I noticed that I was feeling a bit funny, waking up in the middle of the night sometimes with my heart racing. It was a disconcerting feeling, to stay the least.

I went to Ochsner Clinic for a checkup and a conference with the distinguished heart surgeon, Dr. John Ochsner. He did not let me go home. I had 95 percent blockage in the left main artery to my heart and substantial blockage in several others. John Ochsner, a friend since my teenage years, immediately scheduled me for at least a triple bypass, first thing in the morning. As I learned later, I was a "fatal heart attack walking around waiting to happen," seemingly when everything was just fine. How lucky I was to have broken my right big toe three weeks earlier, and Mary and I had stopped jogging the golf course in the mornings. Was He saving me for some greater misery?

Lying in that hospital contemplating life, I knew that I should take the final step into the Catholic Church. I asked Mary to call our friend and pastor at St. Dominic Church in Lakeview, Fr. Victor Brown, a wonderful man, a good family friend, and also my personal friend. Father Brown brought me into the church on that June night in 1979. I was thrilled and deeply moved. Though I am not a daily communicant, over my twenty-seven years as a Catholic, I've missed Mass only two or three times. Of course, Mary takes care of "reminding" me of holy days.

Shortly after Father Brown departed I felt a little tug of conscience and asked for the telephone. I called Billy Connick and told him that I was at Ochsner Hospital awaiting open-heart surgery in the morning. I also told him that I had just joined the Catholic Church, in part because of the good example he had set before my very eyes every day. Nothing can shake the friendship that Billy and I enjoy today; however, during our Superdome Commission days (roughly 1967-72), Billy and I had had a few differences of opinion, although relatively mild for a couple of energetic guys trying to ensure that the Superdome would be the magnificent, extremely versatile facility that it has always been from the day its doors opened in 1975. I concluded my telephone call by admitting that I had always felt that the little differences between us had been at least 90 percent my fault and that I hoped he would forgive me. After hanging up I must have dozed off, because after what seemed like only five minutes, Billy walked into my room. We embraced, probably cried a little bit, said a few prayers together and maybe even a few Hail Marys. We have been close, close friends ever since with a special bond between us that moves me greatly. Billy insisted that our differences were 90 percent his fault, and we settled at 50-50.

Incidentally, Billy and I weren't always feuding during Superdome days. We plotted and planned from my office—actually the governor's office at the State Office Building in New Orleans, which Governor McKeithen had bestowed upon me—the tremendous upset victory for Harry Connick, Billy's brother, over the "invincible" incumbent, Big Jim Garrison. Man, did I learn from that one. In politics no one is invincible. Harry served as district attorney of New Orleans for nearly twenty-five years with much distinction. I am very fond of every Connick I know, and, believe me, there are lots of them. Their numbers test my memory.

After I became a Catholic in 1979, coinciding with successful open-heart surgery, it seemed to me that that Archbishop Philip Hannan had his eye on me, if only because I was invited to so many archdiocesan functions. Actually, I found all of them to be interesting and enjoyable, and very educational to a convert. To my everlasting surprise the archbishop extended to me what I considered the honor of a lifetime, selecting me as lay chairman of his mammoth 1986 archdiocesan capital funds campaign. This was to be the last such campaign of his tenure as archbishop of New Orleans, as he retired in 1988.

I felt that I couldn't decline, but I must admit that I was very apprehensive. As a recent convert I was a little ill at ease at any church function around lifelong Catholics. They were so much more familiar than I with rituals, dates, and history. Moreover, I find it difficult to ask people for money, a reluctance I share with thousands, undoubtedly millions of charity and church workers worldwide. At the same time I knew that somebody must do it. Fundraising, I found, is much like studying in school. Once a person gets started it is not that difficult to accomplish.

The archdiocese had hired a professional firm to advise, teach, and counsel the hundreds of volunteers who had to be out in the field hustling contributions. We must have visited every parish in the diocese. I know that I was amazed at the archbishop's energy and enormous popularity, attracting packed houses everywhere we went. It was easy to give a pep talk to such friendly groups.

That campaign, thanks to Archbishop Hannan's huge popularity, a superb group of volunteers, and the help and guidance of the professional firm we had employed, was a tremendous, record-breaking success, tripling, I believe, the previous record

Dave Dixon greets Pope John Paul II at St. Louis Cathedral, 1992.

Dave Dixon invested into EOHS, a papal order.

and far exceeding our goals. When people would congratulate me on our great success, I would answer truthfully and frankly along these lines: "I really didn't do very much. The archbishop is so popular that everything fell into place for us." If Mary were with me, she sometimes commented, "Oh, he really didn't do anything, it was the archbishop's popularity." Definitely more accurate, but I prefer my version.

One day, a year or two after Pope John Paul II's visit to New Orleans in 1987, Archbishop Hannan told me of the pope's Superdome visit where he spoke so beautifully to 75,000 young people. He later commented to our archbishop, "This is such a magnificent building, so perfect for this occasion. Please rearrange my schedule so that I may stay here a bit longer than the one hour allotted." When I repeated this story to the Superdome's gifted architect, a good Catholic, a tear came to Buster's eye. Without the Superdome, John Paul II could not have visited our wonderful old city, and Buster Curtis and I knew it. A tear came to my eye, too. For me, the Holy Father's visit and that comment constitute the most precious moment in our great Superdome's rich history.

CHAPTER XIV

Tulane Athletics and Tulane University

With the Superdome underway and the Saints energizing the city, my thoughts returned to my alma mater, Tulane, and the university's decades of problems with its football program. It was Tulane that had inspired me as a young sports fan, but the team had consistently fielded losing teams since the de-emphasis of its sports program. I wanted to help in some way the team around which centered so many childhood memories.

Our family home at 7925 Plum Street, where I lived until age twelve, was within easy walking distance of wonderful old Tulane Stadium and the mighty Tulane Green Wave (the "Greenies" as most people called them). So was 1707 Palmer Avenue, our home after I turned twelve. Mother and Daddy went to practically all Tulane games with their friends and frequently took my sister Eleanor and me with them. My sister and I sat in the north end zone wooden stands with thousands of other kids. Moose Charlton and Buck Ware, two first-rate neighborhood guys who were one or two years older than Eleanor, generally were assigned to take care of me, a Greenie fan even at age seven. Admission was 25 cents for kids, a princely sum in those years, compared to a nickel or a dime at neighborhood movie theaters such as the Poplar on Willow Street, a few feet from Carrollton Avenue.

I recall Bill Banker, the Blond Blizzard, an All American running back for the Greenie teams of 1929 and 1930. Believe it or not, football helmets were just coming into universal vogue, but I remember Bill Banker's blond hair, so he must have played without a helmet, at least for a while. Many years later, whenever Pres. Lyndon Johnson good-naturedly kidded Gerald Ford, Michigan's

1932 All American center, famous for playing without a helmet, about "having played one game too many without a helmet," flashes of Bill Banker's blond hair always came into my mind.

Bill Banker stayed in New Orleans after graduation from Tulane, and I got to know him well in later years. Bill once told me that his 1929-30 football teams, mostly undefeated under the great Bernie Bierman, were "bought and paid for." At first I was a little shocked, but I soon understood that he meant that all were scholarship players and paid no tuition. They had to have the grades to get into Tulane, even then.

The 1931 Tulane team, also led by an All American halfback, Don Zimmerman, went undefeated, 11-0, losing a national championship game to a USC team by one touchdown in the Rose Bowl before a record crowd of 90,000, despite gaining more yardage than any team in Rose Bowl history, a record that stood for quite a few years. Tulane was an acknowledged national power during the 1920s, '30s, and '40s until de-emphasis in 1949.

Their huge rival, of course, was the LSU Tigers, located eighty miles up the road at Baton Rouge. In those days everyone in Uptown New Orleans was a Tulane fan, so we all suffered when the Greenies lost, terribly so during the rare years during my boyhood that they would lose to LSU. Most of my little buddies and I knew that Tulane players were "smart" and played "clean" and LSU's guys were "dumb" and played "dirty." I am sure the reverse was gospel in Baton Rouge. In 1932, Tulane, with the great Don Zimmerman, was heavily favored (by three touchdowns), but a flu epidemic wiped out the entire first and second teams. Tulane sought a one-week postponement, which was quickly denied by those "bad sports" in Baton Rouge. The Greenies played with third stringers and intramural players, losing only 14-0. I saw the game with my parents, riding one of twelve special trains carrying Tulane fans from New Orleans, a memorable experience for a nine-year-old kid.

For a long time I never knew anyone who went to LSU, except my older first cousin, Cadet Colonel Frank Dixon McElwee from Centreville, Mississippi. As it turned out, one of our sons, Frank, chose LSU, and all four grandchildren will consider LSU when their days come. Besides, de-emphasis at Tulane and John McKeithen have made a very solid Tiger fan out of me, but not when they play against the Greenies. My boyhood fealty prevails to this day.

It took only a few days after Superdome Amendment #10 was passed into law for me to realize that the Tulane Green Wave had a rare opportunity to make a successful comeback in football, if they chose to do so. They had deemphasized after the 1949 season, thereby committing themselves to losing teams almost every year thereafter and eventually a sad departure from the powerful, lucrative Southeastern Conference. I realized from the outset that eventual demolition of old Tulane Stadium would be a gift from heaven for desperately needed campus expansion and neighborhood tranquility, but I also understood that the Superdome's glamour could become a great recruiting tool for Tulane athletics.

So, I was very pleased to receive a telephone call during the mid-1970s from Dr. Sheldon Hackney, Tulane's incoming president, even before he arrived in New Orleans. His wife's mother, a highly respected citizen of Alabama, and my sister were good friends, and my sister had advised Sheldon that I might be able to provide at least some insight into Tulane athletics. Sheldon's first question was, "What can you tell me about intercollegiate athletics at Tulane University?" "Well," I replied, "for starters, believe it or not, you will inherit a situation where your head football coach, Benny Ellender, and your director of athletics, Dr. Rix Yard, have not spoken to each other for two years." Sheldon was shocked, then asked, "What would you recommend doing about that?"

I hesitated, not having thought too much about the situation. Finally, I said, "I guess I would seek an immediate reconciliation; otherwise I would fire both of them." I explained that the director of athletics, a man named Rix Yard, had a good reputation and relationship with the Faculty Senate, but some people believed it was because he always agreed with faculty and because he had a Ph.D., unique in those days for a director of athletics. I thought highly of Rix, and said so to Sheldon. I liked Head Coach Ellender also, but expressed slight reservations.

Somewhat later, Benny Ellender resigned. I've always had a little feeling of guilt about this situation, as ultimately I concluded that Dr. Yard had forced Ellender's resignation.

Almost immediately, Dr. Hackney asked me to supply a list of names of coaches who might be interested in Tulane. I replied that such a list could be expanded greatly if the question were rephrased. We would compile a list of coaches who *should* be interested in Tulane if approached properly.

The first coach I suggested was Lou Holtz, in 1976 a bright, personable young coach at North Carolina State, where he was doing well after successful years at the College of William & Mary. North Carolina State had played second fiddle for years to the University of North Carolina at Chapel Hill, and I assumed Coach Holtz was a bit frustrated. Sheldon gave me the green light to make a very secret, private trip to Raleigh to see Lou Holtz, who had agreed to meet off campus at a site suggested by him. We spoke for at least three hours, becoming good friends. I knew that the Superdome recruiting potential fascinated him, and I came back with a conviction that a contract of a certain, not unreasonable size would bring this brilliant young coach to Tulane University.

Meanwhile, an interested Tulane alumnus, Buddy Friedrichs, an Olympic gold medal winner and son of a Tulane board member, and I had become friends. We shared an interest in Tulane athletics and the possibility that the Superdome might cure a lot of Tulane's problems in football, provided they wanted those problems cured. It was arranged very quietly at Tulane that I, along with Buddy Friedrichs and Fritz Ingram, a Tulane board member, pretty much my contemporary and someone I knew well, would fly to Raleigh in Fritz's plane on a Sunday afternoon and meet with Lou at his home early that Sunday evening.

Fritz and Lou agreed on terms, and we had a delightful visit for a couple of hours. We shook hands on the deal, and it was agreed that Lou would fly to New Orleans on Wednesday of the following week for a Thursday 10:00 A.M. press conference to announce his appointment as head football coach. We were elated. We felt that we had just hired the best young football coach in America.

Then, Tuesday evening, Lou called me and said that he could

not come. His message was phrased a bit awkwardly, and I asked whether he could not come on Wednesday or whether he could not come to Tulane. He then said, "I'm sorry, Dave. Nothing against Tulane or the deal we agreed to. Maybe some day I can tell you why."

I never did learn exactly why Lou Holtz changed his mind. I always speculated, however, that it had something to do with the fact that Paul Dietzel, the former head coach at LSU, had come to South Carolina (then an ACC member as was Lou Holtz's North Carolina State) as director of athletics. There were rumors that he might return to LSU as director of athletics. I reasoned that if Dietzel were indeed to return to LSU, the last thing he would want would be to have his football coach recruiting against Lou Holtz in such an attractive city as New Orleans, with the Superdome as another powerful attraction for great young athletes and their families.

I like Paul Dietzel, I've always gotten along with him, and, frankly, I would have done exactly what I think he did had I been in his situation. But I couldn't resist the temptation to make this comment to him from a distance of roughly ten feet a couple years later at a Quarterbacks Club meeting shortly after he had indeed come back to LSU as director of athletics: "Oh, Paul, incidentally, I finally figured out why Lou Holtz did not come to Tulane back in 1976." He blushed. I had been bluffing, but his blush told me everything. I don't blame Dietzel, as no LSU coach at that point in time wanted to recruit against a revitalized Tulane playing in such an exciting city and in a glamorous arena.

Unfortunately there had been a front-page comment by prominent Tulane board member Lester Lautenschlaeger a year or two earlier suggesting that Tulane consider discontinuing football. Such a statement, clipped out and saved, would have been great to use against Tulane in any recruiting situation. I'll bet old Paul still has that clipping.

Search Committee

In addition to asking me to make a list of coaches who might logically consider coming to Tulane, Dr. Hackney also asked me to become chairman of a search committee. I knew this would offend athletic director Rix Yard greatly as an infringement on his authority, but Buddy Friedrichs and I figured we could patch things up with Rix, so I accepted.

There were three excellent up-and-coming head coaches of Tulane quality elsewhere whom I knew slightly and who, I believed, would consider a Superdome Tulane, if properly approached. They were George Welsh at Navy, a very competitive person who, I figured, must be sick and tired of losing to Notre Dame by 50 to 60 points. Next was Daryl Rogers at San José State, a very impressive, ambitious young coach. And there was Jim Young at Arizona (not then in the PAC 10), who was doing well at a school that did not have anything close to a Superdome or the excellent facilities the school now possesses.

Sure enough, I was able to get quick commitments to visits from all three. They came in no particular order except schedule availability, Welsh, Rogers, and Young, coincidentally about the way the search committee and I had ranked them.

I was very, very interested in Welsh, with whom I was already conversing by telephone. I felt there was a real possibility that he was the best college football coach in America, as many experts later proclaimed him to be. When he visited, my wife, Mary, produced one of her superb seated dinners — really an elegant dinner party — at our home. Other than Mary and I, those present were Tulane president Sheldon Hackney and his wife, Lucy; Buddy and Susie Friedrichs; George Welsh; Rix Yard and his wife, Skippie; and Clarence Scheps, Tulane vice president/comptroller and his wife. Everything went swimmingly. George Welsh had taken a complete tour of the Superdome earlier with me and obviously was impressed.

After dinner, Sheldon took me, Rix Yard, Buddy Friedrichs, and Clarence Scheps aside and said, "What do we do now? He is tremendous, and he wants to come to Tulane, doesn't he? Shouldn't we offer him the job, right now?" Buddy and I immediately said yes. But Rix Yard said, "No, there's NCAA protocol, and we have two other people coming." Immediately I countered, "Rix, I believe that when you have a sale going, close it.

Besides the next guy won't be here until three days from now, so there's no problem canceling. Let's close this sale." Rix persisted with his NCAA protocol and procedures. We had a near-incident brewing in the corner of my living room.

For weeks prior to this meeting with Welsh, Rix had been leaking alumni interference stories to newspaper reporter Bob Roesler, sports editor of the *Times-Picayune,* identifying Buddy Friedrichs and me by description but not by name. Frankly, I can understand Rix's position, but he had brought at least some of this on himself by his refusal to speak with his previous coach. For that reason Buddy and I deferred to Rix — to my ever-lasting regret — even though we knew our position was correct. All of us had been caught in a circumstance, a brand-new president, ever-increasing media leaks, an understandably disgruntled athletic director, and nonexistent NCAA protocol. We were inexperienced in situations of this type.

The next morning I picked up George Welsh at his hotel. We had a very pleasant discussion, and as we were walking to his plane, I told George that he would be back in New Orleans in three or four days with a wonderful offer to be the next coach of the Tulane Green Wave and his team would play games in the Superdome. "No, Dave. If they were going to offer me the job, they would have done so last night. I sent out plenty of signals that I was ready. Your Superdome is unbelievable," came his reply.

When Welsh returned to his home in Annapolis early that evening, something we could not have anticipated occurred. Waiting there for George were his players, the superintendent of the academy, and an assistant secretary of the Navy to assure George that he would be given the opportunity to recruit better athletes. Under those circumstances George, a Naval Academy graduate, committed to stay. The whole thing was unpublicized and we knew nothing of it.

Two days later, Sheldon Hackney called George to offer him the job. What happened next was typical of George's class. When his secretary told him who was calling, George greeted Dr. Hackney with, "Dr. Hackney, before you say anything to me, I ask that you withdraw my name from consideration. I've decided to stay at the Naval Academy." Sheldon Hackney wished George well and both graciously ended the call.

As he walked to the telephone he must have known that if Dr. Hackney were calling, it meant that the Tulane job was going to be offered to him. It would have been a wonderful ego trip to listen to a great offer from a prestigious university. George showed true class when he put Tulane in the position of not having been turned down.

Losing George Welsh was a huge disaster for Tulane football, as his later record at the University of Virginia speaks for itself. He is retired now, but for at least a ten-year period I think he was the best coach in college football, a belief strengthened by a private, confidential poll of thirty top college coaches who rated George Welsh exactly that way—the best in America—despite his confronting even more difficult admissions standards at Virginia than he would have faced at Tulane. Virginia's stadium seated roughly 25,000 when he took over. It now seats 70,000, sold out for all home games at a school ranked with Tulane academically. Reportedly, Virginia now admits athletes on NCAA standards, which are widely considered to be reasonable and fair, but no cinch.

After losing George Welsh, Tulane pursued Daryl Rogers, the brilliant young coach from San José State. This time the deal was finalized at 2 A.M., after Rix Yard, Buddy Friedrichs, and I met and hammered out a deal with Daryl, who accepted. It was agreed to hold a press conference at Dr. Hackney's office at 10 A.M. that day to introduce Daryl Rogers, impressive in every sense, as the new coach of the Tulane Green Wave.

I arrived at the Pontchartrain Hotel at 9 A.M. to pick up Daryl and his wife. Waiting for me in the lobby was his offensive coordinator, Coach Rivera, who stated, "There's a problem, Dave. Daryl's upstairs right now talking to his wife, trying to calm her down. It seems that she was at dinner last night with a group of Tulane people, when apparently a top Tulane athletic official's wife offended her, and now she doesn't want to come to Tulane. Don't worry, Daryl will prevail in time for the announcement. He's really sold and very enthusiastic." Years later I learned that the offending Tulane official's wife was Skip Yard, a nice person, but apparently a bit outspoken and unpredictable at times.

Well, Daryl didn't prevail, so he and his wife went back to San José. One year later he took the Michigan State job, a Big 10 power, and was very successful. Soon he chose from two or three NFL jobs and became head coach of the NFL's Detroit Lions. Tulane had lost a Big 10, National Football League head coach because two nice ladies apparently had a little misunderstanding.

Our next prospect, Jim Young, had heard about the Welsh and Rogers interviews and promptly accepted the Purdue job. Any coach who knew what happened to Welsh and Rogers would have done the same thing. Coach Young telephoned me as a courtesy and said, "My assistant head coach, a young guy named Larry Smith, is ready for a top job. He's a tremendous recruiter, a good coach, and a good person. You should interview him. I've offered him the number one spot on my new staff, but he wants to be a head coach."

We did interview Larry Smith, along with Gary Moeller of Michigan. Larry, a high-class, very nice young man, got the job, and his performance at Tulane was excellent. He surrounded himself with a first-class staff, several of whom became head coaches at top schools, one in the NFL.

Smith himself eventually left Tulane to return to Arizona, this time as head coach at a school that had been admitted to the PAC 10. He left his successor at Tulane some excellent player talent pretty close to being competitive with top programs. Retired today after a very successful career, he ultimately became head coach at USC, probably the best college coaching job in America. But today's best college coaching job is at Baton Rouge, Louisiana. How is that, coming from an old, unreconstructed Greenie!

The background on Larry Smith's departure from Tulane is interesting. Again, a wife was involved. Larry's wife, Cheryl, had become incensed at the officiating during a Tulane game at Maryland, using some strong, shocking language rather loudly in the stands. Unfortunately, several prominent alumni heard what was said and complained to Sheldon Hackney, who in turn asked Mrs. Smith to visit with him. If I know Sheldon, a very understated, first-rate, kind person, I would guess that his comments to his coach's wife were mild indeed. However, the gossip was that Cheryl was "burned."

Three or four months later, everything had calmed down during the off-season, and all seemed peaceful and quiet at Tulane. About that time, I read a minor three-line story in the newspaper, stating that an investigation was underway at the University of Arizona involving the head coach and football ticket revenues. I thought to myself, "Oh, okay, when the head coach is involved, there is something to this story." While I heard nothing more during the next few weeks, I recalled Cheryl Smith's alleged "burn" and was apprehensive. Very. I was reminded that while women do not coach on the football field, they sure as hell coach everywhere else. Larry Smith had come to us from Arizona, and Cheryl had many friends there.

Meanwhile, Rix Yard had retired, and Tulane had brought in Hindman Wall as director of athletics. Hindman was a good man, very much in charge. Certainly, the day of alumni involvement was over. I, for one, was enormously relieved and pleased after watching one fiasco after another.

One stop in Hindman's career had been at Kansas State where his good friend, Vince Gibson, was head coach. Vince had done a tremendous job at Kansas State, actually beating a number-one ranked Nebraska team at Lincoln, Nebraska. Vince eventually moved on to Louisville, where he did well. But the word now on Vince was that he had lost his zest for recruiting, which can be fatal for a college football coach.

At that moment I dropped Dr. Hackney a note (Mary and I were leaving on a buying trip abroad for our antiques and paintings galleries) making a few predictions, roughly as follows:

1. The Arizona head coach will lose his job, possibly even go to jail. (I believe he actually did serve time in prison.)

2. Arizona will court Larry Smith, whose offended wife will influence him to leave Tulane.

3. Hindman Wall, the new athletic director, will hire his friend Vince Gibson as Tulane's coach, despite Gibson's known aversion to recruiting.

4. Vince Gibson initially will be successful at Tulane (no one

questioned his coaching ability), but dead meat when the lack of good recruiting hits home.

Sure enough, the Arizona head coach was fired, Larry Smith and his wife returned to Arizona, and Hindman Wall hired Vince Gibson as head coach at Tulane. Sheldon told me that he was amazed that I could see those things so far in advance. Actually they were very predictable.

Vince Gibson came as advertised: an excellent coach and an exceptionally bright, entertaining person. He actually gave LSU a fierce whipping (48 to 7) while players from Larry Smith's tenure remained, then got murdered in recruiting three days later on Signing Day. Eventually, the quality of Tulane's teams declined severely, and Hindman and Vince moved on. Vince Gibson remains in New Orleans, a first-rate guy and superb storyteller. He was a good football coach, but Tulane never recovered fully from that recruiting slump.

Incidentally, during my brief, semidirect association with Tulane athletics and the immediate following years, Tulane beat LSU three years out of four, once at the end of Larry Smith's tenure and two out of three by Vince Gibson with Larry's recruits. I cannot help but feel a bit of hard-earned satisfaction.

My Tulane Theory

My belief has been that the Superdome-New Orleans recruiting combination, plus Tulane's own superb credentials and attractiveness, would make my old Greenies a national power again in intercollegiate sports. After all, New Orleans is light years ahead of such places as Starkville, Tuscaloosa, Auburn-Opelika, Oxford, Tallahassee, Gainesville, Fayetteville, and so forth in attractiveness to today's young athletes, not to detract from the charm and lifestyle of college towns and, of course, some fine people and some great state universities. Tulane today seems to be in good hands with Pres. Scott Cowen and athletic director Rick Dickson, so the opportunity is still there for excellence in intercollegiate athletics.

Too, I had always believed that the African-American athletes would come to dominate college football and college basketball. Once the Civil Rights Act was passed in 1964, the flood gates would open in athletics, and ideally also in academics. I have presented consistently to Tulane presidents over the years, really from the days immediately following the completion of the Superdome in 1975 through the presidencies of Sheldon Hackney to Eamon Kelley to Scott Cowen, the glamorous possibility that exists for Tulane athletics. I contend that Tulane could be quite competitive in football and basketball with many of today's collegiate athletic powers simply because of the huge, basic attractiveness of the city of New Orleans and our magnificent Louisiana Superdome to the African-American athletes who dominate those two sports—in addition to the tremendous appeal of a truly splendid institution such as Tulane University.

The recruitment line would be simple: "Young man, where would you rather go to school, New Orleans or Oxford, Hattiesburg, Tuscaloosa, Gainesville, or Athens or such remote, out-of-the-way areas as Fayetteville, Lincoln, Norman, Lexington, College Station, or East Lansing or Iowa City?

"And where would you like for your mom and dad or your grandmother or your girlfriend to be sitting? In an upholstered seat in air-conditioned comfort or on a hard, uncomfortable wooden bench under a blazing sun or in miserable rain or in freezing cold weather?

"Nothing wrong with those remote areas except there's nothing much to do after a big game, any day or night, for that matter. And if you're looking for something to do on a Sunday at Tulane during football season, how about the NFL at the Superdome?

"You won't find the NFL at Tuscaloosa or Starkville or Norman or Lincoln or Tallahassee, and you can't beat the value of a degree from such a prestigious institution as Tulane University!"

And for those student athletes who might find Tulane's rigorous requirements for admission intimidating, Tulane could consider admitting athletes on the basis of NCAA standards, which were nonexistent when Tulane originally deemphasized on that glorious fall afternoon at Gibson Hall back in 1949. I understand that even the University of Virginia, a highly ranked institution academically, admits on NCAA standards. Tulane might then center on character in recruiting, emphasizing that it uses NCAA admissions but takes only young men and young women of top character, so much so that Tulane becomes famous for the quality of its student athletes. I know young people well enough to be very confident that if Tulane were to recruit strictly on the basis of top character and NCAA automatic admission standards, as does UVA, they would be quite surprised and pleased at the results. This character type program could be implemented experimentally with progress monitored very carefully.

Tulane has an excellent, seasoned new head football coach in Bob Toledo (of UCLA fame) and an attractive director of athletics in Rick Dickson. They might welcome the chance to be truly competitive, but they must also be held strictly accountable so that recruits are indeed first-rate in character, no exceptions.

With good recruits, Tulane could once again be competitive and draw very, very well with top teams that Tulane followers know will not beat them by 30, 40, 50, or 60 points, whether an Alabama or an LSU. Tulane in New Orleans and in the Superdome could win an occasional game against such opponents and do quite well against Ole Miss, Mississippi State, Vanderbilt, Southern Miss, Memphis, Houston, SMU, or TCU.

Being competitive on the playing field will turn $5 million deficits into $5 million surpluses. That's a $10 million difference right there. Tulane almost certainly would attract at least two to three thousand additional affluent, qualified student applicants per year, students "able to pay their own way" despite the high price of a Tulane education. Assume that Tulane would accept one thousand such new applicants per year. Such an increase in revenues would be welcomed at any great academic institution in America.

In conjunction with a revitalization of Tulane's sports program, why not a Tulane-Loyola joint venture to acquire a first-rate, on-campus arena seating 7,500 to 8,500, ideal for athletics and for attracting top-quality entertainment events? I've thought ahead to the details of splitting and sharing usage and even to the location. It seems feasible, and I actually suggested this while a member of the Loyola Board of Trustees roughly twenty years ago. It is probably much more feasible today. Two great universities should be able to work out the details.

A joint venture would be unique, but where else are two fine universities physically located side by side as closely as Tulane and Loyola? A shared arena would generate a natural, friendly rivalry in basketball and other sports and a site for social activities among next-door neighbors will have been built. It would provide great PR for both universities, maybe the beginning of a great new era, helping both universities attract top-notch students. I'll bet my last USFL football that a select study committee dedicated to helping each other to become even greater universities could be successful beyond someone's wildest dreams. Tulane University and Loyola University are two huge, huge community and regional assets. Not including the draw from Uptown, Loyola's 5,500 students plus Tulane's 13,000 would create a ready-made 18,500 market for on-campus entertainment, athletics, and social events. A reinvigorated New Orleans following Katrina would respond with great enthusiasm. Make certain, though, that you announce it to the world as part of the renaissance of a wonderful old city.

Will Tulane ever seize the opportunity its credentials, its location, and its use of the Superdome present? No, I don't think so. It never has in my adult lifetime and I have had a very lengthy adult lifetime. Besides, I have seen no zeal or real determination by either the university president or the athletic director for Tulane to be competitive in intercollegiate athletics again.

But, who knows, it might be fun competing against similar institutions such as Rice, SMU, and Tulsa. Winning can be fun. So is being competitive. Consistently losing is not. Of course, if circumstances, fate, and certain individuals had not intervened, and if Lou Holtz or George Welsh or Daryl Rogers had actually coached at Tulane, or if Larry Smith and his great offensive coordinator, Lindy Infante, had not moved on, how different would things have been? Whatever the university does athletically, we are fortunate indeed to have such a great educational institution in our midst. I must say that the various associations at Tulane were immensely enjoyable and leave me with great feelings about Tulane University, a superb institution.

CHAPTER XV

The United States Football League

One of the most interesting and demanding experiences of my lifetime had to have been creating, organizing, and bringing into reality the United States Football League (1983-85), the only serious challenge and rivalry that the NFL has faced during its modern history. The USFL was a twelve-city major professional football league that played its games from March through July in top cities and stadiums across America: same game, different season, with no preseason practice games at full price, as in the NFL.

Seven people were of huge assistance to me in putting the USFL together. Four of these enormously valuable helpers were my wife, Mary, and our three sons, Frank, Shea, and Stuart, the latter one of the best "idea guys" I have known. Always of invaluable assistance, either Mary, Frank, or Shea traveled with me on most USFL organizational trips. Shea, a Stanford- and Tulane-educated attorney, was league counsel during the organizational period and attended league meetings with me. Frank managed our business interests at home but also went with me fairly frequently when we were searching for owners. Our fifth invaluable source of assistance was the Stanford University and Denver Broncos former head coach, John Ralston, a tremendous friend to all Dixons. A sixth was Ed Garvey, head of the NFLPA, the NFL players' union, who educated me to pro football, a solid friend to this day. The seventh — Fr. Jim Carter — helped bring about a miracle.

Football is known as a fall sport, so we were defying tradition by playing in what is primarily the spring. But I did reason correctly that football is known as a "fall sport" simply because Rutgers and Princeton played their famous "first game" of football in the fall, and the sport took off from there. If those two great institutions had played their first game in the spring, the chances are football would have become known for its spring tradition.

The NFL begins its season in ideal weather and ends during bitter cold months. Our USFL would begin with a couple of games in cool but good weather, ending with perfect weather. Weather-wise, the USFL was superior to the NFL. Our confidence even to this day in a spring-summer schedule was to be solidly validated by USFL experiences. Football in America is king, anytime, anywhere, never think otherwise. No wonder John McKeithen always said that recognizing that fact is akin to a political wisdom.

One of our earliest USFL owners was to have been Donald Trump, the highly publicized, actually delightful New York real estate developer and entrepreneur. I must have had a dozen or more always interesting visits with "The Donald" over the years. I liked Donald twenty-five years ago, and I like him now. Donald's first huge success was buying the old Commodore Hotel, located at Grand Central Station in Manhattan. He completely gutted the Commodore, retaining only the steel structural framework, and emerged with the brilliant Grand Hyatt, a great financial success. One of our first league meetings occurred at Donald's new hotel while we were very much in a preliminary phase of the USFL, not yet formally organized. At an earlier organizational meeting at another location, several uninvited persons had attended, offering only disruptive and useless ideas for other sports or other leagues. To prevent such interruptions at this meeting, we had a strict rule that all prospective owners could gain admission only if they posted a check for $5,000 and signed a strictly worded agreement that the deposit was nonrefundable, dedicated to a league organizational purpose.

I put my charming, very dependable wife at the door to collect the $5,000 checks and signed admission agreements. This was a successful stratagem that gave the USFL a huge head start by eliminating any "nuts" from applying, facilitating much better, more organized meetings. Only one serious potential owner (all had agreed in advance to this new procedure) showed up without a $5,000 check. That person was Donald Trump, ironically in his own hotel.

Mary stood at the door, not budging one inch, blocking The Donald's entrance. Within five minutes Donald's secretary rushed over with his nonrefundable check for $5,000, which he signed on the spot and gave to Mary. Donald was gracious, stating to our group, "Maybe we've found our commissioner." I was very proud of Mary, for the one-millionth time, but Donald was right. She would have been a great commissioner, far and away better than the two high-priced commissioners who eventually presided so ineptly over the USFL.

At the meeting, Donald Trump agreed to be our New York owner, but at a very late date he backed out (apparently the NFL sabotaged us), throwing the league into a bit of disarray at the last minute. Fortunately, some last-minute reshuffling saved the day for our ever-changing USFL. Walter Duncan, the splendid Oklahoma oil man, had been scheduled to be our Chicago owner, close to his beloved University of Notre Dame at South Bend, Indiana. Walter brought his longtime friend, Chuck Fairbanks, who had won national championships, or near championships, at the University of Oklahoma to be his head coach. Chuck had also coached for the most part successfully in the NFL at New England and was extremely helpful to our league during its formation and organizational stages. Somewhat reluctantly Walter Duncan agreed to take the New York franchise, promptly naming his team the New Jersey Generals because their games were to be played at Giants Stadium in the Meadowlands of New Jersey, the only suitable football stadium in the New York area. Walter eventually sold the Generals to Donald in 1984.

George Allen, the great old Washington Redskins coach (famous for the phrase "the future is now"), and his team owner, the world-famous heart surgeon Dr. Ted Dietrich, from Phoenix, agreed to move to Chicago where George years earlier had coached so successfully with the Bears while assistant head coach to George Halas, the true, much admired patriarch of the NFL. I loved Mr. Halas, "a great American," as John McKeithen had earlier described him so accurately. Finally, a part owner of one of our teams, Jim Joseph, agreed to become owner at Arizona. Jim Joseph completed our lineup of twelve founding owners.

But, oh boy, it had taken almost two full years of tough, bone-wearying travel and hard work to reach that point. Indeed, toward the end of our owner-seeking efforts, I had visited with our friend Fr. Jim Carter, president of Loyola University, telling him that I had eight owners as "definites" and four as "maybes." I had confided to Father Carter that I was worn out by constant travel and frustration, and that I probably was going to throw in the towel if any of my Solid Eight defected and if two of the "maybes" did not materialize. Besides, my stamina was not the best, as I had undergone triple bypass heart surgery in June 1979.

The next day Father called to say that he had a dozen Jesuits praying for me and that he had a wonderful feeling that every-thing was going to work out for Mary and me. Almost immedi-ately I got word that one of our Solid Eight, Alex Spanos, the largest builder of apartment complexes in the world and our owner-to-be at Los Angeles, had bought a 10 percent interest in the NFL's San Diego Chargers, eventually becoming 100 percent owner, as he is today. So Alex was out. Fortunately L.A. was the only place where we had a "standby," and within the hour I had successfully replaced Alex Spanos with Bill Daniels, the famous cable TV pioneer. Replacing Alex had taken just one good phone call. Then, two of our "maybes" called to say that they were in, both outstanding, very strong business leaders. Now we were at ten really good founding owners. The next day our two remaining "maybes" came through.

It was like a miracle. We had spent nearly two years chasing prospective owners all over the universe, then within a three-day period, we replaced one owner and received a "go" from four "maybes," completing the owners' roster. Alleluia!

I give my great friend Fr. Jim Carter and his fellow Jesuits full credit for their miracle. Those Jesuits were my seventh great helper. For me the USFL became "The League That Faith Built." If we had properly publicized that theme and the story behind it, the USFL might be flourishing today. I still regret the fact that we didn't hang the slogan "The League That Faith Built" on our USFL. The Jesuit miracle would have made nationwide reading and listening. Why do I have such great ideas months or even years later? Ah, hindsight.

The irony of the Jesuit miracle is that I had spent countless schoolboy hours cursing the Jesuit High School Blue Jays with my worst teenage words because they always seemed to beat my Fortier Tarpons with last-second heroics. Luck, I called it at the time. Come to think of it, isn't last-second heroics what the Jesuits did for me so many years later? How times change. Today, I'm a big Blue Jay fan. Jesuit High School and Loyola University of New Orleans are both great institutions; they make miracles in education happen daily. I actually go to Jesuit high school football games every now and then. Still great entertainment.

Thus, we were able to assemble twelve financially sound founding owners, all in top markets. The East supported the New Jersey Generals of New York, the Boston Breakers, the Philadelphia Stars, and the Washington Federals. In the Middle West, there were Detroit's Michigan Panthers and the Chicago Blitz. In the South, we had the Tampa Bay Bandits and the Birmingham Stallions. The Western teams were the Denver Gold, the Arizona Wranglers in Phoenix, the Los Angeles Express, and the Oakland Invaders.

The networks and ad agencies loved our brilliant lineup of cities, demographically and geographically, and I believed that we would get important TV contracts simply because the breweries and auto manufacturers had told me that football was their best advertising medium and that they would welcome the USFL. So it was no surprise when the USFL received attractive offers from ABC and ESPN, ABC's then brand-new all-sports cable network, as well as NBC. Fox was not yet in existence, and we had no chance at CBS, which was snugly in bed with the NFL, who promptly dumped them the next time the networks got a chance to bid on airing the games, an example of the vagaries of loyalty NFL style. But that's business. Our owners chose ABC/ESPN, although several of us, thought we should have worked a deal with NBC for at least part of our TV package. Otherwise, we would have no leverage. Mistake number one.

At a USFL special league meeting shortly after completing our formidable lineup of founding owners and top cities, our owners chose between our two top league-commissioner candidates, Chet Simmons, then the first president of ESPN, and Jim Finks. I voted for Jim Finks, former president and general manager of the Chicago Bears, outstandingly qualified for the position after a long and distinguished career in the NFL. A majority of our owners, intelligent guys, voted for Simmons, mistake number two. There were two likely reasons for such a decision. Our USFL owners were basically inexperienced in TV and in football. Chet Simmons was "experienced" in TV — though he had garnered mixed reviews, by my information — having held seemingly influential executive positions at two or more networks, but always there was no record of real accomplishment. Nevertheless, a majority of owners seemed to think that he would be helpful in attracting TV bids. I, however, knew that my sons and I had already persuaded NBC and ABC (owners of ESPN) to bid for our TV rights, so unfortunately, Chet added nothing in the way of TV. The second reason for the owners to have chosen Simmons over Finks was decisive, I believe. Jim Finks was a terrible smoker, smoking one cigarette after another while we were meeting with him. I heard at least two or three owners comment about his excessive cigarette use: "Did you notice how many cigarettes he smoked while we met with him? He won't live three or four years, poor guy. Lung cancer or a heart attack will get him for sure."

With the newly appointed commissioner, Chet Simmons, residing and after a highly publicized announcement ceremony at the famous 21 Club in New York City, our first official league meeting occurred at the Washington Hilton in D.C. All thirteen owners were present. I was the owner at Houston, a non-activated franchise, but a voting owner on all league matters, as contractually agreed for my having put the league together. In addition to the thirteen there must have been thirty to forty non-owners in the meeting room, assistants to various owners and unidentified hangers-on. Who knows, maybe an NFL spy? At any rate, there was much confusion.

Something that could have been a major catastrophe occurred

New York City press conference announcing the USFL, 1981.

immediately. The commissioner incredibly opened the floor to an owners' open discussion of salary caps, league-wide limitations on players' salaries. Unintentionally, he was inviting the owners to break the law in front of witnesses. Instantly, I made my way to the commissioner's chair and whispered to him to clear the room of all except voting owners, which Steve Ehrhart, an able assistant to the commissioner, a good man and a lawyer, did rather quickly and efficiently. Incidentally, Steve has done a superb job making the Memphis Liberty Bowl game into a first-class success. I'm proud of him. If Steve had been our commissioner we might still be playing. I then asked to address the owners and made a brief statement along these lines: "Gentlemen, I'm no sissy. I'll talk about almost any subject at any time, but salary caps is a very delicate topic, quite likely a serious antitrust problem if not handled with great discretion, which is why our commissioner has cleared the room of all except voting owners.

"But let me tell you something that might be the solution to our problems. Courts have held that agreements reached after arm's length negotiations with a labor union are generally exempt from antitrust restrictions on topics covered within that agreement." Indeed, the NFL has such an agreement with its union, the NFLPA, as of this moment. That is exactly how, at long last, they are controlling players' salaries, free of anti-trust worries.

I continued: "The head of the NFLPA is a gentleman named Ed Garvey with whom I've had an ongoing relationship as I put together this ownership group. I talked to Mr. Garvey again this morning by telephone before coming to this meeting, and I have really good news. He told me in effect that the NFLPA is so anxious to have a viable alternative to the NFL that they would agree to what would be an extremely attractive deal for our USFL. His offices are just across the street from this meeting room. He'll come over to give us his ideas, if we wish. He's very bright."

Sitting not five feet away was one of our top owners, an enormously successful developer, and always very cordial and friendly toward me. Immediately, my friend said, "A union? What are you, Dave, some kind of communist?" Everyone laughed, as did I. To this day, I do not know whether this otherwise courteous and famous gentleman was kidding or not. At any rate, it appeared to me that all NFL owners thought they knew better than to sit down and discuss the inviting proposal that Ed Garvey was willing to make. "A union, hell, we'll bust any union" seemed to be the attitude of the majority. Little did they know what a mistake they were making. The result was excessive player salaries that eventually led to the USFL's undoing. Mistake number three. Three strikes, you're out? Sure enough, these super-motivated entrepreneurs apparently had already lost all sense of payroll discipline, and signed all their linemen to excessive salaries, a direct result of owner ego gone awry. Owner ego, absolutely the mortal enemy of any sports league, had taken over.

I was already planning to sell my rights to Houston, and I think I made up my mind at that moment to visit promptly with prospective buyers there. After a couple of weeks of on and off negotiations, I sold my USFL franchise rights to a top Houston person. As a result Mary and I were able to make a substantial gift to Loyola University in deep gratitude for all those good Jesuit prayers.

There were many comical instances of runaway ego in the USFL. For example, the league's opening weekend in late March 1983 was typical, spread over several time zones and different days. I believe that I made at least five openers in different league cities. At the last opener Mary and I arrived midway through the first quarter due to travel delays. We went to the owner's suite at a beautiful stadium, where we were greeted very nicely by the owner's wife, a charming lady but someone who to my surprise had never been to a football game. I asked where her husband was, and she said immediately, "Oh, our telephone to the bench is not working, so he went next door to the coaches' booth to use their telephone to tell our coach to change quarterbacks." So help me, that's a true story.

At a later USFL stop for the Michigan Panthers, I rode to the game with their general manager, who told me their story. "We've lost our first three games by a total of five points, mostly freak plays, so our owner asks, 'What the hell is the matter? My

Dave Dixon, USFL New Orleans team owner Joe Canizaro, Randy Vataha, and Coach Dick Coury, 1983.

Dave Dixon holds USFL football for Gov. Edwin Edwards at announcement for the league's New Orleans Breakers, 1983.

friends at my club are riding the hell out of me. It's embarrassing. I don't like to be embarrassed, particularly at my club.'"

The Michigan general manager continued, "Actually we're a good team. Maybe we could be a little stronger at offensive line. My owner then said, 'Get one,' so I go out and sign three NFL offensive line starters, all free agents, including two from the Pittsburgh Steelers. With any luck at all, we'll win the league championship, even though we're 0 and 3 right now. We have a great, super-smart young quarterback, Bobby Hebert [of later fame with the Saints] and a spectacular wide receiver in Anthony Carter [the University of Michigan superstar]."

Sure enough, the Michigan Panthers with superior talent went on to win the USFL championship game, a high-scoring thriller, over the Oakland Invaders, a low-budget team coached by my super friend, John Ralston, the great former head coach at Stanford and the Denver Broncos.

Despite the problems caused by what I saw as the overarching ego of the league owners, we had put together quite a football league. To demonstrate the quality of play, ten years after the USFL ceased operations the NFL's Outstanding Offensive Player of the Year was the San Francisco '49ers' Steve Young, earlier of the USFL's Los Angeles Express. That same year the NFL's Outstanding Defensive Player of the Year was the Philadelphia Eagles' Reggie White, originally from the Memphis Showboats of the USFL. Both NFL Most Valuables in one year were former USFL guys.

We had other top-notch player talent such as Herschel Walker, Jim Kelly, Anthony Carter, Sam Mills, Marcus Dupre, and Bobby Hebert, who enjoyed a highly successful career with the New Orleans Saints and later with the Atlanta Falcons. I know and admire Bobby. He is very intelligent with a great sense of humor. One of my favorite Saints ever, he is already a great hit as one of Buddy D's successors on WWL radio in New Orleans.

These excellent players were playing in the most impressive lineup of founding cities and owners of any football league in history, strategically divided across the East, the Middle West, the South, and the West. We had access to fine stadiums everywhere, as antitrust law ensured stadium availability for the

USFL in all NFL cities (a bit of legal research confirmed by my lawyer son, John Shea Dixon), even if several were necessarily baseball parks. Our teams were led by excellent coaches—George Allen, Marv Levy, John Ralston, Steve Spurrier, and Jim Mora.

And, of course, the USFL received first-rate TV coverage with ABC and ESPN. The league games got off to a great start, an incredible 14 rating on ABC the first weekend, higher than NFL ratings. The USFL consistently rated higher than major league baseball and the NBA whenever head to head on network TV, averaging a highly acceptable 6.1 rating over three years—ABC made millions—and a record 3.0 cable rating for more than one USFL telecast, a cable mark that stood for years. Moreover, the USFL was ESPN's top-rated programming for years. In fact, ESPN executives readily admitted for years that the USFL made ESPN. Again, football is king!

Average attendance, always with no blackouts, was 26,000 over three years. Using a Pete Rozelle formula, employing sensible ticket-sale requirements before allowing telecasts, our USFL, according to Pete's calculations, would have averaged roughly 47,000.

As we progressed into 1984-85, the USFL's major problem was that almost all franchises were losing money, sometimes big money, despite the league's enormous popularity. Teams were paying too much for players, a malady brought on by individual egos. The one exception was my very intelligent friend Ron Blanding, with the Denver Gold, who operated on sensible budgets and stuck to them. Ron turned a profit every year and was very competitive. I repeat, ego is the mortal enemy of any sports league owner. The USFL ultimately failed—no question about it—because of that three letter little word, as my intuition had warned me at that Washington, D.C. meeting in 1982 when our owners shunned that NFLPA offer of an agreement that would have saved them from themselves. It ruined our USFL, that and perhaps NFL intimidation of the TV networks.

In 1986 the USFL filed a lawsuit against the NFL, claiming that its monopoly harmed the league and that the NFL was pressuring networks not to air USFL games. Donald Trump's showboat attorney, one Harvey Meyerson, won the league's antitrust lawsuit against the NFL but "forgot" in his closing statements to the federal jury hearing the case to mention dollar damages suffered. What a tragic oversight, unfortunate for the USFL and for football in general, if you believe, as I do, that there is no such thing as a good monopoly. Abuse is inevitable.

Having already decided that the NFL was guilty of antitrust actions against the USFL, but having no knowledge of what damages should be awarded, the jury decided that "the judge would straighten things out" (according to their own statement) and awarded $1.00 in damages, perhaps the strangest antitrust verdict in history. I have a framed copy of the NFL's check payable to the USFL for $3.76 ($1.00 in damages tripled under antitrust law to $3.00, plus interest of 76 cents). Thanks to Steve Ehrhart, the capable former assistant to the USFL commissioner, for my copy. No one has ever explained to my satisfaction why that judge did not send the jury back to decide sensible damages and why subsequent courts of appeal have acted similarly.

Some USFL owners said that the NFL's political influence was widespread and powerful indeed. Perhaps that trial was still another example of the urgent need, even today, for an NFL competitor. "Those guys [the NFL] got away with hundreds of millions of dollars of antitrust violations," said my USFL owners. I was not present at any sessions of the trial, as lawyers from both leagues had asked me to testify in their behalf.

Having won the antitrust suit but losing any hope of monetary help for the league, which was floundering in debt due to owners' mismanagement and poor leadership, the league had no choice but to fold before beginning its 1986 season.

How Georgia Lost Herschel Walker, The True Story

The Herschel Walker of 1982 might well have been the finest college football player of all time. He was everything a coach or a parent could want, blazing speed, heroic strength, "smarts," and great character, a genuine legend and a gorgeous young man. Only one or two of us in the USFL knew that Herschel, a junior at the University of Georgia, planned to sign with an agent as early as the day following the 1983 New Year's Day Sugar Bowl national championship battle matching the University of Georgia and Herschel Walker against Coach Joe Paterno's Penn State team at the Superdome. Penn State won 27-23 in an epic battle, giving Joe Paterno his first undisputed national championship, richly deserved.

The day before that classic match-up we polled our thirteen owners by telephone to ask, first, whether the league should sign Herschel. He had one remaining year of eligibility at Georgia and would be the first college junior in history to sign a pro contract. Second, we asked which USFL team should be designated as the one to approach Herschel's agent. The league owners were unanimous with a go-ahead. They also were unanimous in stipulating that the New Jersey Generals would have first shot at Herschel for maximum overall benefit to the league. If Herschel did not want to sign with New Jersey, Los Angeles and Chicago would be next in line. Absolute, total confidentiality was pledged by each USFL owner. To my amazement, they really did stay quiet.

Within a very few days following the Sugar Bowl, Herschel signed with the New Jersey Generals, receiving huge publicity nationwide. The USFL was on its way to the big leagues. I was very proud and pleased.

As Herschel's signing was made public, all hell broke loose, particularly in Athens, Georgia. When the news broke that Herschel had signed with us, most of the Georgia coaches were vacationing following their heartbreaking 27-23 Sugar Bowl defeat by Penn State. Their head coach, Vince Dooley, who was in Honolulu, flew home immediately, determined to pull Herschel away from the what Coach Dooley described as the "evil" clutches of the USFL. The owner of the New Jersey Generals with whom Herschel had signed was nationally prominent, tremendously successful independent oil producer Walter Duncan, Jr., a great friend of college football in general and the University of Notre Dame in particular. Walter was a person of impeccable reputation, kind, considerate, a distinguished Catholic layman, perhaps as good a man as I have known—far from "evil."

When Coach Dooley arrived in Athens after a grand vacation with visions (now ruined) of a second national championship attempt featuring his superman, All Time All-American running back, Herschel Walker, he and his staff really unloaded on Walter Duncan, as quoted in every newspaper in America. Mr. Duncan and the USFL were portrayed as "evil," and Herschel as "naïve," misled by "bad" people. Undergraduates at that time always had completed their four years of eligibility before signing with the NFL, which, in this instance, was already posturing as the paragon of all virtue, but they were also upset with all the publicity now being given to a potential competitor, the USFL. As always, I was amused by my friends in the NFL. Until Herschel Walker they could find tons of laws that made their requirement of four years of college eligibility appear to be legally sound. Suddenly, after Herschel signed with the USFL, all of that changed. The NFL now finds all kinds of law that justify a three-year requirement.

In hindsight, I think it was all of us — the Georgia coaches, the USFL owners and I, the general public, and the Bulldog supporters — who were naïve. I believe that Herschel thought when he first read of the USFL in 1982 that it could be a wonderful opportunity for him. Averaging forty or more runs per game, his body was likely taxed and exhausted. He knew he could not go to the NFL at that time because they would not take anyone with less than four years in college, but as a junior, he probably wouldn't improve greatly his senior year. Figuring that his Georgia team had a great chance to be national champions that year, he decided to sign with the USFL at the end of the year and make some real money instead of suffering all that pounding he would take as a senior at Georgia without making any money. So, he decided to find a good agent and get some advice, but not sign with him or any agent until after his team's last game, which he hoped would be the Sugar Bowl in New Orleans. That way, if they won a national championship, no one would be able to take it away from him, his teammates, or the University of Georgia. Herschel had this whole thing figured out perfectly, well in advance. He carried it off brilliantly. Did Herschel confide or insinuate those things to me years later in a weight room at the Minnesota Vikings headquarters? No comment.

Finally, Herschel himself, despite the validity of his well-thought-out plan, and under great pressure back in Athens, Georgia, had a change of heart and publicly declared that he wanted to remain at the University of Georgia. He actually telephoned Mr. Duncan and asked to be let out of his contract. Unfortunately for the University of Georgia, the Georgia staff continued to pour invective on a now bewildered Walter Duncan. One particular printed insult, a direct quote, offended Mr. Duncan terribly. He telephoned me, quite nonplussed, saying, "David, I'm very upset. Herschel is such a nice young man, and you know how I feel about college football. He has asked me to let him out of his signed contract, which I was about to do when I read in the papers and saw on TV the latest insults from the Georgia coaches. I've never been so offended, and I now plan to stick to the contract. Besides, they're running that wonderful young man forty times a game. He'll be worn out by the time he's ready to earn the first significant money of his lifetime. Is there any way we can end all this controversy?"

I asked, "First, Walter, are you absolutely sure that you want to keep Herschel?" When he said yes, I advised him that Herschel was permanently ineligible under NCAA rules to play any more college football at Georgia, or anywhere else. Having signed a contract with a player's agent, he was ineligible. If a newspaper printed that fact, the controversy would be all over.

Walter seemingly almost jumped through the telephone. "For goodness sakes," he sputtered, "His agent participated at the signing. I have a friend, a top writer with the *Boston Globe*, who would be delighted to get such a scoop. I'll call him right now."

I warned, "Walter, in all fairness, Herschel took great pains not to sign anything with anybody until after Georgia's final game so as not to taint or jeopardize their national championship possibility. He's a very high-class young man. Make certain that your writer friend makes that point in his story. Vince Dooley and his staff might be doing the wrong thing to you right now, but let's do the right thing by them today." That was the end of our telephone conversation.

The *Boston Globe*'s late Will McDonough handled the story exactly as requested. Coincidentally, Will and I had been good friends for many years (I set him up for tennis whenever he came to New Orleans). I knew that Will was trustworthy, and I said so to Walter Duncan.

Herschel Walker himself had made absolutely certain that he was not under contract before Georgia's final game of the season. I admire him greatly, and he did the right thing by the University of Georgia.

There is one more little anecdote to the Herschel Walker-USFL signing story. It is Coach George Allen's aborted effort to recruit Herschel Walker for his Chicago Blitz of the USFL. George Allen came to New Orleans for that New Year's Day 1983 Georgia-Penn State national championship Sugar Bowl, fully hoping and perhaps expecting to sign Herschel for his Chicago Blitz, even though he had agreed with everyone else in the league to let the New Jersey Generals take first crack at Herschel because of the New York exposure for the league. But that was George, a gifted coach, always looking for an edge. We had great midfield seats, George and I, about halfway up in our magnificent Louisiana Superdome. Until that day I had suspected that old George somehow had already signed Herschel, but this assumption would turn out to be incorrect.

On one play Herschel on an end sweep came running almost exactly in the direction of our seats in the Superdome. He was pursued by at least six Penn State guys, all as big or bigger than Herschel, and it was obvious that a huge collision was about to take place. Sure enough, it ultimately took all six Penn State guys to get Herschel down, and he ended up with the six huge tacklers on top of him. I looked at George. He was pale as a ghost, obviously concerned that his future superstar had been hurt. It took almost a full minute for the officials to get all six Penn State players off Herschel. Finally, there he was, prone on the Superdome floor, pancaked.

I looked at George again, who was seemingly impassive, except that his Adams's apple now was moving up and down, almost out of control. I've never seen such an Adam's apple, either before or since. Herschel just lay there, motionless, still flat as a pancake. Suddenly he jumped up and raced back to the Georgia huddle. He had been "resting." George relaxed immediately, and his throbbing Adam's apple quit throbbing. On the very next play Herschel ripped off a twenty-yard run, brushing off one tackler after another, and George jumped to his feet. What a physical specimen Herschel was, the strongest and the fastest running back in America. At this point I was still confident that George had already signed Herschel to a Chicago Blitz contract, but George's secret quest of Herschel was not to be.

George Allen

Many football fans and businessmen will remember George Allen as the coach about whom Bennett Williams, the famous Washington attorney, and George's owner when George was coaching the Washington Redskins, once said, "I gave George an unlimited budget, and he has already exceeded it."

We had a somewhat similar experience with George. At a certain point in 1982 we felt that Donald Trump needed just one more little nudge to become our New York-area USFL founding owner, so I gave George a $2,400 personal check for round-trip, first-class air fares for himself and his wife, Etty, to go to New York to convince Donald to join with us. We found out later that good old George never did talk to Donald about the USFL, but George urged Donald to buy a particular NFL franchise and make him, George, the coach. That is why Donald Trump did not come into the USFL until our second season (buying the New Jersey Generals and Herschel Walker from Walter Duncan). Regardless, George more than made up for my Trump disappointment, later playing a key role in helping to put the USFL together. As a coach he also contributed greatly to the USFL's recognized excellent quality of play.

After the USFL disbanded George apparently retired from coaching, concentrating on being chairman of Ronald Reagan's National Physical Fitness Board. President Reagan at George's request, made me a member, so I attended meetings, always at George's elegant quarters in Beverly Hills.

About that time I noticed that Mike Ditka, head coach of the Chicago Bears, seemed to be slipping each year after the Bears' incredible 1985 season (talent assembled by Jim Finks). So, I asked George about football coach Mike Ditka. I'll never forget his answer. Cracking his knuckles, much as Captain Queeg in the film *The Caine Mutiny,* George Allen's reply was one for the ages: "Mike has only one weakness. He can't coach." That's like saying that a surgeon can't cut, or an accountant can't add.

But old George could not stay away from coaching, even well into his 70s, becoming head coach at Long Beach State, winless for two years, holders of the nation's longest losing streak. George made them a winner right away, actually going to a bowl game, which he won. He was a helluva coach. Shortly after that final game, George, who was a physical fitness addict, running miles every day, always in great shape, handsome, still restless, contracted pneumonia and died very unexpectedly. His wife and three children, all of whom obviously adored him, were crushed.

Months later I was in Los Angeles on business but met also with Bruce Allen, George and Etty's youngest son, now general manager of the Tampa Bay Bucs. I wish him well, except when they play our Saints. Bruce and I had dinner together, and his mother, Etty, joined us, talking about old USFL days and other nice memories. After dinner, Etty showed me the route that she and George ran together almost nightly. Then she said something to me that I will always remember: "I still run at night, and sometimes when I come to a vacant area where no one can hear me, I let out my emotions and just scream, I miss George that much!" That story reminded me so much of my own grief when, at age fifteen, I lost my father. I still scream on very rare occasions. Etty exposed, in effect, one of my deepest personal secrets.

A Future League

As I finished writing this chapter on the USFL I began to realize an enormous truth that will be essential to any future football league, if there ever should be one. It would be a league that would equal or actually exceed the NFL within five to six years. I know now exactly how to do it, but at this age, I am not certain that I will have the energy and drive necessary to bring it into being and to make it strongly profitable from year one of operation.

It has become part of my daily thinking, very tempting, so maybe you will be hearing soon of the spectacular new football league now fermenting in my mind. I think of it as the perfect football league. We might even call it that, the PFL. More likely it will be named the Fan Ownership Football League after its driving concept: fan ownership.

CHAPTER XVI

The Saints' Modern Era

People who have known Saints owner Tom Benson the longest and the best speak highly of him. A person of excellent character, they say, pretty much a daily communicant at historic old St. Louis Cathedral. Incidentally, a visit to St. Louis Cathedral, a beautiful, inspiring old building, can be very rewarding. It is reported that Tom Benson has been a generous parishioner. Good for him.

Benson is a native New Orleanian, one of the top automobile dealers in America. He got his start in the car business with Mike Persia at old Mike Persia Chevrolet on North Rampart Street, about three blocks from Canal Street. I knew Mike Persia fairly well. Eventually, Mike sent Tom to San Antonio to manage his Chevrolet dealership there. It wasn't too long before Tom was able to buy out Mike Persia in San Antonio. The rest is history. He was a major success in San Antonio as a Chevrolet dealer, gradually building a collection of well-run, profitable car dealerships there, in New Orleans, and elsewhere. Today he is mostly retired as an automobile man, retaining his Mercedes dealership on Veterans Boulevard, plus one or two others. Still a top notch car guy, he is a very, very active, hands-on NFL owner.

Tom Benson saved the New Orleans Saints for our city. No question about it. John Mecom, Jr., had decided to sell the Saints as his father's oil empire gradually disintegrated during the early 1980s. To his credit John did not quickly accept a strong offer from Jacksonville, Florida, business interests, instead giving various New Orleans groups the time and opportunity to keep the Saints here, if at all possible, which in all candor was also because the Mecoms were still heavily invested in Louisiana oil properties.

It was Tom Benson during late 1985 who eventually assembled the funds to meet Mecom's price. Tom was not a football man, but this New Orleanian is a sound businessman, and he correctly saw the Saints as a huge business opportunity. His first move was to hire Jim Finks as his general manager. Jim Finks was available at that moment because he had resigned as president and general manager of the Chicago Bears when Mr. George Halas, Sr., their great owner, elderly by then, wanted to hire Mike Ditka, one of his former players to be head coach of the Bears. Jim did not think that Ditka was head coach material. He was, of course, correct. Jim had done a masterful job as president-general manager of the Chicago Bears in assembling talent, feeling by the mid 1980s that the Bears, with good coaching could "win it all." Neill Armstrong, struggling a bit, was his incumbent coach. When Mr. Halas, a great man in my book, insisted on hiring Mike Ditka, Jim Finks resigned as a matter of principle.

I knew Jim Finks well from NFL meetings, from his great years as general manager of the Vikings. His Vikings played a pre-season game for our New Orleans Pro Football Club, Inc. in the summer of 1966. I even remember him as an excellent college quarterback at Tulsa, I believe. Most of all, I remember when Jim interviewed for the commissioner's job of the United States Football League (the USFL), of which I was the founder. The other finalist was Chet Simmons, founding president of ESPN (rumored then to be on his way out). I had known Chet Simmons while he was with ABC, attending NFL meetings, perhaps for three or four years. The choice between Finks and Simmons really was no contest, Jim Finks was so clearly superior. It is likely that if we, the USFL, had hired Jim as commissioner the USFL might still be playing. Jim Finks was a very able football executive. I had sold my USFL franchise in Houston to an investor there in early 1983, so I had only a brief look at Chet Simmons, but what I saw, combined with earlier impressions, was not favorable. Personally, a very nice man and a good person, but a commissioner? He was not even close to being qualified to be commissioner of a major sports league.

On the other hand, I had always been impressed with Jim

Finks, aside from those damned cigarettes he smoked so heavily, so I was enthused when Tom Benson almost immediately hired Jim, who in turn, hired the best football coach from the disbanding USFL, Jim Mora of the Philadelphia Stars, USFL 1985 champions. Mora was the best coach, by far, at that point in Saints history. Jim had been highly successful with the Minnesota Vikings and the Chicago Bears, a solid football man with a great eye for talent, liked and respected across the entire NFL. Universally admired, actually beloved within the NFL, he was a very sound choice.

It was ironic that I already was well acquainted with Jim Mora. It gives me satisfaction that the league I put together brought the first semblance of respectability to our New Orleans Saints. Those great linebackers, Vaughan Johnson and Sam Mills, quarterback Bobby Hebert, and Coach Jim Mora raised the level of professionalism and talent on the team.

When the 1986 NFL season began, the New Orleans Saints were really not much better than an expansion team, suffering badly from the inconsistent direction of the Mecom days. Tom Benson, Jim Finks, Jim Mora, and the USFL's former players quickly changed things for the Saints, promptly turning them into a formidable NFL contender. Right off the bat, Benson-Finks-Mora gave us respectable, competitive football, the first in Saints history. But this was not to endure.

During the history of our New Orleans Saints there have been four very unfortunate occurrences, listed chronologically, which together have made second-class football citizens of the Saints over the years. The Saints' troubles began with John Mecom, Jr.'s appointment and selection as founding owner of the Saints from 1967-85. John was a non-resident who spent little time in New Orleans. He was much too young and inexperienced in business and in life for such a serious responsibility. I assume my share of the blame for his initial selection, as discussed earlier.

Under Tom Benson and general manager Jim Finks, the year-long holdout of Bobby Hebert in 1990 and his eventual loss as a free agent starter to the Atlanta Falcons was a major mistake. Jim Finks, probably due in part to failing health, mishandled Bobby Hebert's holdout, leading to Bobby's sitting out an entire year. In declining health, Finks underestimated Hebert's determination to obtain a contract commensurate with his skills and his four-year record as a first-rate Saints quarterback (1986-89). Bobby Hebert became a free agent, then signed with our big rival, the Atlanta Falcons, leading to consistent Saints losses to the Georgia team.

Hebert's move led eventually to the terrible trade for Steve Walsh of the Dallas Cowboys. The Cowboys' coach, Jimmy Johnson, and their owner, Jerry Jones, had suckered a physically failing Jim Finks. Walsh simply was not close to being an NFL quarterback, and Jim Finks in good health would have known better. Bobby's market value? Probably a high first-round draft choice, maybe two first-round picks. The Saints got nothing for him. A huge loss. Walsh did not have an NFL arm, plainly, and he cost the Saints dearly. Jim Mora knew very quickly, I think, that Walsh did not have an NFL arm. Moreover, his presence created dissension within the Saints ranks.

Now the Saints, after a promising start with Finks-Mora, were in trouble. Hebert was in Atlanta and Walsh was inept, an extremely expensive failure, a total Saints disaster. When cigarettes completed their toll on Jim Finks, who died from the inevitable emphysema and lung cancer, Coach Jim Mora suffered badly from a lack of direction, eventually leading to his resignation, though he reestablished himself as an excellent coach with the Indianapolis Colts.

After Jim Finks' untimely death, in 1994 Bill Kuharich became Saints general manager. Bill is a fine human being, but obviously not a judge of coaching talent, for it was he who led Tom Benson into the Mike Ditka trap. It can be said, then, that the presence of Bill Kuharich and Mike Ditka in top Saints positions constituted our third and fourth unfortunate occurrences.

I can understand what happened, as I knew Ditka fairly well through several meetings and discussions with him. Mike had brought a well-qualified Chicago owner to me for the league I came very close to putting together during the mid-1990s, to be called the Fan Ownership Football League, based, obviously, on eventual fan ownership by thousands of stockholders in each league city. Mike Ditka was a very convincing, likable guy on a one-on-one basis, but not a good football coach. He sounded like a great coach, a great leader. He spouted impressive clichés. "Smash-mouth football, snot-nose football, suck it up!" were Ditka's favorite expressions. Sounds great, but he took a terrific team, the Chicago Bears of 1985, and coached them into losing. The opinion that he was a poor coach was widely held by every knowledgeable football person known to me (except one, my friend, Buddy Diliberto), in particular the famous old Redskins and USFL coach, George Allen, and locals Archie Manning, Peter Finney, and Jim Henderson. This was also a common belief among Mike Ditka's coaching brothers. Mike was a good, dynamic person, a fiery competitor, but he had been fired for losing—no other reason—by the owners of the Chicago Bears, despite his great popularity among fans and Chicago media. Mike Ditka was a player-winner but, for our Saints, a coach-loser.

Unfortunately for Tom Benson, there were four huge liabilities for Ditka as a head coach. He played way too much high-stakes golf, gambled substantial sums at casinos, was not a hard worker, and eventually wrecked that great '85 Bears team. Moreover, anybody who plays for big stakes at casinos cannot be very bright in my book. Or possibly addicted, just as bad. I noticed, too, after the '85 Bears won their Super Bowl at the Superdome that the Bears players rushed up to Buddy Ryan, their great defensive coordinator, and carried him off the field on their shoulders, not Ditka, their head coach.

Mike Ditka is a charming, delightful, entertaining guy, an attractive conversationalist, and an incredible competitor as a player. Mike Ditka charmed Tom Benson. Some people say that Bill Kuharich saved his own skin as general manager, persuading Benson to sign Ditka and then later re-sign him and Kuharich, both at huge salaries. I knew Saints general manager, Bill Kuharich, and his family. They are first-class in every respect, as was his father, Joe Kuharich, a beloved figure in the Rozelle years of the NFL. I am certain that Bill hoped against hope that Mike Ditka, fired for losing by the Bears, would suddenly become a highly successful coach and everyone would live happily ever after. That was not to be. Indeed, I remember talking to Archie Manning and Peter Finney on the day of the announcement of Ditka's hiring. I was shocked and dismayed and expressed that feeling to Archie and Peter, both of whom shared my view, even more strongly. People who knew football knew better, definitely. Bill Kuharich should have known better. The situation was actually very reminiscent of Mecom's hiring of the great Hank Stram, whose best coaching days by that time were clearly behind him.

I had been horrified at the Ditka signing, shocked that such a solid, experienced person as Benson would not check out Ditka very, very thoroughly. If Tom Benson had made such an investigation, he would not have hired Ditka, and he would have fired Kuharich for recommending him. It was as simple as checking with the Bears to confirm the reason for his dismissal. How could an NFL owner not make such a check? Is Tom Benson overrated as a tough, smart businessman? Perhaps, but probably confined only to football matters. It was his lack of football knowledge that led him to the sad decision to hire the former Chicago coach. Benson's mistake in hiring Ditka without a careful check was a terrible blunder that set the Saints back eight to ten years.

Those four things—the ineptness of the Mecom years; Jim Finks's tragic illness, which probably led to his mishandling of Bobby Hebert's contract and Bobby's departure for Atlanta; the subsequent, suckered-in trade with the Cowboys for an unproductive Steve Walsh; and ultimately the hapless Bill Kuharich-Mike Ditka regime—all combined to create the uncertainty we faced in 2004 and 2005. Those were major, self-inflicted wounds for Tom Benson, a good man in my opinion but one who does not possess even a good fan's knowledge of football, a serious shortcoming. We have put the Ditka era behind us.

So in 2000, the Saints under new direction went to Jim Haslett as coach and the bright young Randy Mueller as general manager. In 2004, the Saints had finished strongly, particularly in the final game at Carolina when a playoff berth seemingly was at stake. And I repeat here my often expressed view: Aaron Brooks is an excellent young quarterback, in raw talent one of the best in the NFL, but mishandled. He could be a winner elsewhere.

Possibly even as big a winner as Bobby Hebert became for Atlanta during the 1990s. The next year, 2005, was a crucial year for Jim Haslett, but Katrina took away Jim's last chance. Personally, I think Jim Haslett was the second-best coach in Saints history. I wish him good luck with the Rams.

The 2006 hiring of Sean Payton and Mickey Loomis's acquisition of Drew Brees was a stroke of genius. At long last I see a better future for our New Orleans Saints. In 2006, we had one more indication why John McKeithen described knowing that football is king as a great political wisdom. The Saints in early May drafted Reggie Bush, the "star" of the NFL's 2006 Draft Day. So Tom Benson, just a few days earlier a community villain, had become a community hero, receiving a standing ovation from hundreds of Saints fans four days later as he entered the room at Saints Headquarters where "The Welcome Reggie Bush Party" was taking place. Football really is king, particularly with a 2006 standing ovation for Tom Benson in New Orleans, Louisiana. Given the circumstances, I would have participated in the standing ovation for Tom Benson myself. So, too, would have Buddy Diliberto.

But, if John McKeithen were here I'd tell him my biggest, most surprising prediction of all: Tom Benson will emerge after our first Super Bowl victory as the best liked person in the history of our great city . . . and stay that way. He's on his way now, believe me. I see a mellowing Tom Benson very clearly. Don't smile, I already note those first signs everywhere. Old Tom is mellowing. He has Mickey Loomis and Sean Payton, and I have known for a long time that a true New Orleanian exists beneath Tom Benson's sometimes dour countenance. Moreover, I like old Tom, and he knows it, primarily because he is one of us. As a matter of fact, Tom smiled when he greeted me on that great Monday night at our Superdome. A "first." A tiny smile, but a smile! My first from old Tom! Tom Benson, I must say, is maturing as an owner, a maturation process helped along by Reggie Bush falling into our laps. I see gradual improvement ahead, slowly, year by year, but clearly discernible. Besides, I am an eternal optimist about every aspect of our wonderful old city.

Buddy D vs. Tom Benson

Despite the rocky record of the Saints organization, the team had no greater supporter than the late Buddy Diliberto of WWL Radio in New Orleans. When you live eighty-four years on this earth you know five or six people whom you would rate as highly as I rated Buddy, but there was no one I liked and respected more. He was the best sports talk-show host in America, honest, accurate, well-informed, highly entertaining, and tuned into this market and its people exactly. Yes, I enjoyed listening to his show, but I liked him because he was so honest and such an enjoyable guy to be around.

One huge point that Buddy and I definitely had in common was a love of sports. He was the biggest sports fan I knew. The greatest object of his affection as a sports fan was the New Orleans Saints, by far. That is also my number one interest in sports, so we have shared much agony over the years and pitifully little ecstasy. Buddy and I suffered together through the early years of the Saints. Believe me, nothing could have been more frustrating than the nineteen seasons of watching the Saints of John Mecom, Jr. Terrible coaches and general managers almost without exception. There were a few capable men here and there and a handful of outstanding players, foremost of them all, Archie Manning. Great player, great person. No wonder Archie and Olivia fought so hard to help their son, Eli, dodge the difficult Spanoses in San Diego. Archie and Olivia had "been there and done that" with the Saints.

Buddy came to life when Tom Benson bought the Saints from John Mecom, Jr., and in 1986 promptly hired the Saints' first top general manager, the great Jim Finks, also a first-class person. I came to life, too. Buddy D was pleased with this promising new Finks-Mora regime. At last "his" New Orleans Saints were to be a factor in the NFL after all those terrible Mecom years, which weighed even more heavily on Buddy than on me, or so he claimed. I don't know about that; I have suffered mightily over the years with the Saints. Mary, for example, will go to Saints games only when and if they improve, which they did in 2006, dramatically. I will go until I drop!

Though Buddy was an ardent, dedicated fan, like all Saints followers, he had moments of frustration and disillusionment as a result of year after year of losing seasons. For Buddy D, there was only more frustration when, with a general manager who had seemed so promising, Tom Benson mishandled an internal crisis during Randy Mueller's early tenure, leading to the departure of Mueller, who, of course, had handpicked Haslett. Again, the Saints had a coach without his mentor or partner, in a sense repeating the situation experienced with an ill, dying Jim Finks not being available to his coach, Jim Mora. Buddy D then became disenchanted with Jim Haslett, leading to Buddy's state of despair regarding the Saints and Tom Benson, which lasted until Buddy's sudden death in early 2005.

I shared most of Buddy's feelings, but I was not sure about Jim Haslett. I believed that the 2004 season would be critical to his fate as coach of the Saints. The pressure in 2004 was on for everyone: for Jim Haslett, for the Saints as a whole, for Tom Benson, for Buddy D, for thousands and thousands of devoted fans. Even for me. I was optimistic, yet very apprehensive as I looked at corners, linebackers, and the offensive line, without Willie Roaf and Jim Turley.

Late in the 2004 season Buddy D spoke his mind in what amounted to a radio editorial, delivered in a moment of despair, rooted in the frustrations of the helpless, hopeless, hapless Mecom years, the ever-too-brief, tantalizing flashes of brilliance during the Finks-Mora years, the same emotions with Mueller-Haslett, and finally with the departed Randy Mueller, the newest Saints duo becoming in the negative minds of many Saints fans a Benson-Haslett duo. Buddy's impatience was understandable considering one little playoff victory in thirty-eight years, nothing even close to a Super Bowl appearance until a year after Buddy's death in January 2005. Buddy's late-season radio editorial set off a nine-alarm fire, a furor at Saints headquarters. What he said was essentially that the only recourse for years and years of frustrations for Saints fans was simply not to buy tickets, which was painfully straight to the point. Though it was pretty sound advice already being followed by many thousands of ex Saints fans, it was probably not a very constructive suggestion.

According to an eyewitness report (I still had sources), just about every Saints top gun at Airline Drive called WWL management, complaining all the way to New York (or wherever headquarters of the conglomerate now owning WWL Radio is located). Local WWL management apparently considered a one-week suspension, then a three-day suspension, finally settling on a one-day suspension, still later changing their minds a fourth time. Well, I knew my boy, Buddy D, pretty well, and I say that even a one-hour suspension would have caused Buddy to walk away, to resign.

Had that happened, the Saints would have been "mauled" by listeners, a public relations disaster of the highest degree for the Saints and for WWL Radio—and perhaps for the First Amendment. Buddy D was exercising his First Amendment right, guaranteed as freedom of the press to news media. Did the Saints regard WWL Radio as simply a propaganda outlet for themselves? Buddy's integrity, his freedom to tell it like it is, would have been challenged publicly, and the huge losers in public opinion would have been WWL Radio and the New Orleans Saints.

Maybe Buddy was too strong when he suggested that the fans' only alternative was to refuse to buy tickets, but he was speaking as a long-suffering fan, an honest fan. He was speaking the truth. Lawyers would have lined up to handle a Buddy D lawsuit against WWL and the Saints. Fortunately for all, Buddy was not the suing type.

Of course, Buddy was on the wrong side at times. Who hasn't been when it comes to the Saints? Buddy had shared a radio show from a Bay St. Louis entertainment and casino center over a period of many months with Mike Ditka, the former football coach who had been fired by the Chicago Bears for losing, for dissipating the enormous talent Jim Finks had assembled and that had produced their powerhouse Super Bowl championship team of 1985. The Chicago Bears won that game 46 to the New England Patriots' 10 in the Super Bowl here in New Orleans. Mike Ditka is entertaining and a great conversationalist, so I can understand why Buddy, exposed to Mike for several hours, one-on-one, week after week, would think this guy was the perfect answer for our New Orleans Saints.

Tom Benson, too, is a good man in many respects, some unseen by the public, but what the public sees is also Tom Benson. For a time after he hired Finks, who hired an excellent football coach and a good person in Jim Mora, I thought we were lucky to have him as an owner. But Tom apparently does not understand the art of effective public and human relations, which makes him a difficult owner. A Moon Landrieu or an Archie Manning, for example, would never have gone screaming to WWL Radio about Buddy's editorial during 2004. In fact, I understand that several Saints executives participated in the attempted lynching of Buddy D. When going outside the organization, only one voice should be heard in situations of this type, not four or five.

If the Saints had good, competent public relations they would be light years better off in their relationship with the New Orleans public. I am told that they do have good PR advisers — at one point Arnie Fielkow was performing various duties for the Saints, but in 2007 he entered politics to become a member of the New Orleans City Council — but Tom Benson does not listen to them. He should, for a Buddy D suspension and resignation would have been a total disaster for all concerned. Believe me, in 2004 such a suspension would have spread the idea of boycotting Saints games to several hundred thousand additional team followers. It would have cost all principals a ton of money and would have been a huge, huge PR catastrophe for the Saints and for WWL Radio and a lawsuit bonanza for Buddy D. Come to think of it, who was the chump (or chumps) at WWL Radio who even mentioned the word "suspension"?

Though my friend Buddy D might have skipped the suggestion about not buying tickets — that wasn't his finest hour — the guy, as always, was remarkably attuned to his audience. There was tremendous frustration out there with the fans of our New Orleans Saints during 2004 and the Hurricane Katrina 2005 season. That was not Buddy D's fault. It's Tom Benson's fault. He is the owner, and the buck stops there. However, Tom blames the city and its people (a great way not to sell tickets), everyone except himself.

All of this was avoidable. Buddy Diliberto was a good guy, a very good guy, a magnificent person, one who would have listened to a courteous, reasoned response. Instead, individual Saints officials were put in the untenable position of bulldozing or bullying one of the top media people of this area by going directly to station management personnel, in effect, putting Buddy on the spot, trying to get him severely reprimanded. I assume that Buddy D's shows made a lot of money for WWL Radio. So WWL management was put in the delicate position of balancing a superbly talented employee against the New Orleans Saints. No one was happy with the inevitable triangle: not Buddy D, not WWL Radio executives, not the New Orleans Saints. There must have been a better way to do things than to bully Buddy Diliberto.

The Saints needed then and need now to have one individual in charge of public relations. And his name is not Tom Benson. This is one of the few weaknesses in Tom Benson's armor. Tom's PR skills desperately need fine-tuning, as he does not understand the nuances of top level PR, or see the need for it.

Oh, Buddy D vs. Tom Benson? Buddy Diliberto by a technical knockout. Buddy won every round, at least in public opinion!

A New Orleans Team, Today and Tomorrow

Even with Tom Benson as owner, the Saints will never leave New Orleans. The NFL will not desert a stricken—or an "unstricken"—New Orleans. As explained in earlier pages, I regard Tom Benson as a good man, a good human being, but a difficult owner. His lack of football knowledge and his personal PR shortcomings can be overcome, but to date, regrettably, his performance as an owner can be considered only moderately good, a possibly overstated rating. Yet the people of New Orleans have supported the Saints magnificently, with easily the best attendance per victory of any NFL club in history, making it a cinch to set the record for attendance per playoff victory, with one exception.

It is not Tom Benson, but Paul Tagliabue and his successor as commissioner, Roger Goodell, who are the reason New Orleans will never lose its NFL franchise. Not a chance now, almost no chance in the foreseeable future. I have known for years that Pete Rozelle's successor as NFL commissioner, Paul Tagliabue, is a person of rare and tremendous capabilities. I have noticed carefully his concern for his players, for their futures, and for the game's high injury rate and his efforts to address those problems. He is very, very bright, and I know now that it is of extreme importance that leaders of government and industry should possess great personal intelligence and solid, good character. This NFL commissioner has those qualities in abundance. Those leaders who lack the right intelligence fail at their duties. There must be the right mixture of "smarts," compassion, practicality, and toughness. Goodell seems to be cut from the same cloth.

Tagliabue is a good, conscientious person who would never kick a great, wounded old city such as New Orleans when it is down. Second, as the brilliant young legal adviser to Pete Rozelle, he had to have become familiar with the fact that it was New Orleans, through Hale Boggs and Russell Long, that responded so quickly to commissioner Rozelle's fervent appeal to me for help with the NFL-AFL merger bill, then locked hopelessly in committee, destined to die of old age until Hale Boggs' rescue. Yes, Hale Boggs and Russell Long rescued that bit of legislation, making near-billionaires out of today's NFL owners. The NFL owes New Orleans, and the commissioner knew it, as does Roger Goodell, an impressive person and a twenty-year veteran at NFL headquarters in New York.

If somehow the NFL franchise is taken away from our city and state, it would be a despicable, unprincipled act on the part of the NFL that would warrant congressional action and a monstrous antitrust suit that would cost the league dearly. Paul Tagliabue is too good a human being and was too competent a commissioner to have allowed the NFL to be seen as a bullying enterprise that must be brought to heel. He also knew that if the NFL in a moment of total stupidity had allowed Tom Benson to move to San Antonio, or anywhere, that New Orleans lawyers would race to the nearest federal courthouse to file multibillion-dollar antitrust lawsuits against the NFL. The NFL would be in mortal danger of losing such a lawsuit the moment a jury heard a top lawyer proclaim that the NFL would plunge a dagger into the back of the great, wounded, old American city that saved their AFL-NFL merger bill forty years ago. The NFL owes New Orleans an eternal debt.

Of course, Benson's expressed desire to move the Saints out of New Orleans stems from his numerous failed attempts to persuade the state to finance a new stadium, one that would replace the Superdome as the home to the team. He began his years of negotiations with state officials around 2001, when Mike Foster was governor. What little I saw of this recent governor, I liked. I am confident that Foster, whose two terms in office lasted from 1995 until 2004, was 100 percent honest, and judging from a distance, I think he handled the Tom Benson-New Orleans Saints stadium matter fairly well. He could not give and did not give Tom a new stadium, which would have been ludicrous, even disgraceful, but he did work out what amounts to an extremely generous small-market subsidy. Clever guy, Tom Benson, he made Mike Foster "look good" and then settled for what he wanted in the first place. Then, on October 20, 2004, Gov. Kathleen Blanco wisely ruled out a new stadium.

It is difficult for me to make a first-hand judgment of Mike Foster, as I never really saw him in action. I was excluded as a member of his fifty-five-person Blue Ribbon Stadium Committee, reportedly blackballed by Tom Benson (the compliment of a lifetime?), denied even the opportunity to express my views to that august group. That exclusion was ironic, as I would have suggested and supported a very small, small-market subsidy that I believed then was the real Saints objective — but definitely not the size of the subsidy that Benson eventually negotiated. Moreover, as a French Quarter merchant I could see firsthand the impact of the economic downturn that was occurring prior to 9/11, and I would have suggested a cautious view concerning hotel tax revenues, which today are below original expectations.

Though he did not get what he wanted from the state, Tom Benson came out of this latest controversy somehow smelling like the U.S. Mint. The thirty-one other NFL owners each chipped in one million dollars to a Tom Benson Relief Fund for clever old Tom to behave himself.

CHAPTER XVII

The Final Chapter

I cannot close this book without one small, additional chapter. The 2006 rebirth of our magnificent Louisiana Superdome before a nationwide TV audience, the biggest in the history of Monday Night Football and ESPN, was not merely the accomplishment of a lifetime for the heroic Doug Thornton, the chief executive of the Superdome Management Group (SMG), which operates the Supredome for the Stadium Commission, and his valiant Superdome staff and all who worked so hard for so long. Their activities during that dreadful period during Katrina already are legendary. Nor was the stadium's rebirth symbolic only of the dedication and hard work of the the omnipresent, ever watchful and dedicated Tim Coulon, chairman of the Louisiana Stadium and Exposition District, or of Louisiana's resolute Gov. Kathleen Blanco. As I stated at the outset of this work, I think it was much, much more. I believe strongly that it was a magnificent victory for the great, indomitable human spirit that exists in all of us, the spirit that drives New Orleans, this truly unique, treasured old city of ours.

Fortunately, it was also a wonderful victory for our spectacular new head football coach, Sean Payton, and for a great Saints general manager who selected Sean Payton so carefully, so skillfully, and so expertly, still an unsung hero, Mickey Loomis. Coach Payton will take us to three victorious Super Bowls before I move across the street to Metairie Cemetery. For the first time ever I am strongly optimistic about our Saints. The "new era" that my four staunch, civic-minded friends Edward Poitevent, Bobby Monsted, Sonny Westfeldt, and Hugh Evans and I had thought we were creating for our city back in 1961 has arrived at long last.

Watching the 2006 Saints in their opener at Cleveland forty-five years after I set out to bring the team to New Orleans in 1961, I remarked to my wife at some early point in the game, "My word, sweetheart, I see several signs of a well-coached football team!" Mary laughed.

Then, the next week, during the early going at Green Bay when the fumbling, bumbling Saints handed the Packers 13 free points—would have been 21 with the "old" Saints—miracle of miracles, our Saints rallied and won.

Oh, but I thought, surely Michael Vick, our special, elusive nemesis, and the Atlanta Falcons on national TV in our heroically restored Louisiana Superdome would bring back the "same old Saints," much loved, but losers. Nope, the Saints won handily. Could these guys actually be the "new" Saints? Yes, indeed, they certainly seemed to be the "new" Saints on that wonderful Monday night, September 25, 2006, at our magnificent Superdome. However, whether I talked to friends or to strangers during the 2006 season, it seemed that all of us confessed to the same negative, almost amusing thought whenever a moment of adversity arose (a fumble, an interception, a long touchdown run or pass by the opposition). It was, "Oh, my God, have the old Saints returned?" I admit readily that on each negative, early occasion, such as the three quick turnovers at Green Bay in Game Two, my reaction was, "Damn, these guys are the same old Saints." But I didn't turn off the set because I had seen moments during the opener at Cleveland that I hoped were not mirages or my imagination; the team appeared to be well coached. All of us know now that it was not a mirage; we were indeed looking at a well-coached Saints football team, but we were also mindful of the all-too-brief Jim Mora era and those USFL additions.

Ah, but every old-line Saints fan somehow "knew" as the Saints traveled to Dallas that the ultimate humiliation awaited us against the despised, supreme NFL bully, the Dallas Cowboys, on Sunday night, December 10, on national TV. They were a red-hot Dallas team led by the masterful coach Bill Parcells. Sure enough (was it just the second play from scrimmage?) some clown in a Dallas uniform runs 77 yards, or something like that, for a Dallas touchdown. So easy! It was immediately obvious to us old-timers that these were the same old Saints. And, then, a little later we mess up a punt and get penalized back to the 10 yard line. "Ninety yards to go," I thought to myself. "It'll be Dallas, 14 to 0, in just a few minutes. So damned frustrating!"

Then, a wild intuition hit me like a ton of bricks, and I said to Mary, "Watch these guys, sweetheart, they are going to march 90 yards for a touchdown." To my amazement, Mary said, "I have the same feeling!" How's that for a couple of wild, powerful intuitions? Oh, did I enjoy that beautiful, un-Saints-like drive of 90 yards. Let's call it a Payton-Brees-like drive. How sweetly the game ended: the New Orleans Saints 42, the Dallas Cowboys 17. "Pulled up, laughing," as they say at the racetrack.

These guys have proven that they really are the "new" Saints, no matter what happens from here. Sean Payton, Drew Brees, Deuce McAllister, Reggie Bush, those tough, beat-up defenders, our superb receivers, our defensive ends, those offensive linemen, our suddenly elusive fullback, all of them. I stand with my earlier prediction that Tom Benson will rise to the status of civic hero, and Buster Curtis 's magnificent Superdome will be with us for many, many more years than Mary and I have left on this earth.

A Super Bowl victory for our Saints? Another impending national championship for our LSU Tigers? You better believe it. I do.

But the big story for Saints fans now is that the "old" Saints are done and gone, a thing of the futile, frustrating past. Every Saints fan I know believes that the "new" Saints will be with us for many years to come under the triumvirate of Tom Benson, Mickey Loomis, and Sean Payton. No question about it, our Saints are in good hands, at long last. Almost all of us believe today that the "losers" of the past have become the "winners" of the present and the future, not to return to the "old" Saints in the foreseeable future. As long as that "triumvirate" is intact, particularly that Sean Payton. So, the important lesson of 2006 is that almost all of us believe or "know" that our New Orleans Saints will be a well coached team in 2007 . . . and for many years to come!

That's what this wonderful old city has deserved for forty years or more. This is what I thought or hoped we would get when a great New Orleans mayor, Chep Morrison, made me his Major League Sports Committee chairman in 1961 and what I hoped we would get as I described my vision of a Louisiana Superdome to John J. McKeithen, who so emphatically said to me in early 1965, "Mr. Dixon, that Superdome you just described to me will be the greatest building in history, and, by God, we'll build that sucker!"

And John McKeithen made certain at my suggestion that the magnificently talented New Orleanian, Nathaniel C. Curtis, Jr., was selected as chief architect over every top architect in America. What a job Buster Curtis did! A genius of an architect, a genius of a person.

Thank you, too, Tom Benson, thank you, Mickey Loomis, (I knew that guy was a good man before he even arrived here), and thank you, Sean Payton. What a coach! Thank you, too, and good luck to all our heroic Saints. Plus the best football fans in America! At long last, the promised land in football is coming here to make its long-term home in our great, wonderful old city of New Orleans. Today in New Orleans, the best football fans in America welcome our "new" Saints to the toughest, most indomitable city anywhere in the world, and home to the Super Bowl champions of a very near year to come! Thank you, New Orleans, Louisiana. Together the Saints and New Orleans have overcome difficulties in the past. We've faced years of losing seasons under John Mecom, lived through years of rotating coaches and erratic leadership under Tom Benson, and excelled in the face of the nation's worst natural disaster, one that took our homes and briefly muted our city's spirit, but the team, like its city, has a soul, one that will strive and excel. Most of all, as I close this book, I love my wife; my sons Frank, Shea and, Stuart; my four grandchildren Elexa, Zach, David, and Madeleine; and all the people of the great city of New Orleans and of our great state of Louisiana. With all my heart.

A New Orleans (and Louisiana) Afterword

I've never been able to touch it, I can't find it, I certainly cannot see it or talk to it, but somehow, somewhere, I guess that I've always believed that New Orleans uniquely is a city with a soul. Yes, a city with a soul! It's out there somewhere. I sense it strongly. I have shared my thoughts on this subject with numbers of people, and I have an unbroken streak of agreements that now numbers at thirty-four. I stopped at thirty-four because I know now that anyone who would disagree simply is not from here. Whether the discussion is with the city's respected judges or a friendly stranger on the street, the response they give is usually, "Oh, I've always felt that way, and somehow or other every member of my family agrees. This city is different, I know it, I sense it, I feel it. Maybe it's because we're an old city, but, yes, it does have a soul. Hell, yes!"

There is something mystical about the city, tied to its people, who bring the spirit and the faith and the inexplicable uniqueness that makes New Orleans what it is. Whether that spirit is of a religious nature or a community nature, this grand old city has a soul, somehow, somewhere, and that is what makes its people strong enough to overcome adversity on the football field or at the hand of brutal nature.

And it is this spirit that colors those truly exceptional New Orleans individuals, what I call its "icons." These citizens are widely known, usually native born or so much a part of the city as to seem like natives. They have been so productive over so many years and admired, indeed loved, by thousands of New Orleanians. In no particular order here is one man's opinion of local icons, all living except two, for if I were to include during my own lifetime the deceased among New Orleans icons, the list would be very long indeed. It would have begun with Dr. Alton Ochsner, the great surgeon, founder of the world-famous Ochsner Clinic and Ochsner Foundation Hospital, and included Kitty Duncan, the brilliant, persuasive, civic-activist whose imprint is everywhere at Audubon Park and who did, indeed, "Save Our Zoo."

1. Fire Chief Bill McCrossen. Bill McCrossen was one of those rare individuals whom you meet only briefly but come away feeling that you know that person well on just the one encounter. At least that was my personal experience. He, of course, was an open book. What you saw was what you got. What you got with Chief McCrossen was a great fire chief, a dedicated public servant who served our community superbly.

2. Archbishop Philip M. Hannan. Archbishop of the Diocese of New Orleans from 1965-89, Archbishop Hannan is age 94 as we enter late 2007. The whole archdiocese is rooting for this dedicated priest to make 100. What a celebration that will be! I want very much to be in attendance for such a great day.

3. Buddy Diliberto. My good friend Buddy D belongs in this august company. An individual who rooted for his hometown every day of his life, Buddy was waiting along with me for a Saints Super Bowl team. I hope I will live to see that day although Buddy won't make it to a Saints Super Bowl in physical presence. Several mourners have predicted he is already lobbying the Halls of Heaven for such an occasion.

Some of us regarded Buddy as a "character," a New Orleanian who murdered pronunciations spectacularly, as many of us do, but I compare him with the best of his trade elsewhere. A consummate professional, he was most of all someone who was widely loved and admired by the people of his hometown. Incidentally, out of respect for this wonderful, dedicated human being, I never asked him to pronounce the name of the manufacturer of the car he drove. But, yes, it was a Mitsubishi. One night he actually said over WWL-Radio, "I drove away in my Mister Beezness." If Buddy isn't a New Orleans icon, who is? Nice to everybody . . . except "squirrels" . . . and Saints owners!

4. Angela Hill. Like Buddy, Angela Hill is the best at her trade

Dave Dixon and Buddy D at Buddy's roast, 2005.

of anyone I have seen and heard anywhere. As far as I am concerned, she the best female co-anchor in America. My wife, Mary, thinks Angela will be the perfect eulogist when I drift off to that great Superdome in the sky (hopefully, that will be the direction I'll be drifting).

5. The Manning Family — Archie, Olivia, Cooper, Peyton, and Eli. How can I leave out any member of this family? The three sons, Cooper, Peyton, and Eli, are all natives, but I think of Archie and Olivia as natives too. That's the finest compliment I can pay this eternally young, beautiful couple. It's no accident that their sons handle their own hard-won fame so modestly, gently, and graciously. Those are just a few of the many virtues Archie and Olivia have passed along to their famous sons.

The first day I met Olivia she let me know that Philadelphia, Mississippi, her hometown, is far superior to Archie's Drew, Mississippi. This adopted New Orleanian said, "Philadelphia is far more advanced than Drew. We have two traffic lights, plus several parking meters. Drew doesn't have any of either." How can one argue with such beautiful Mississippi logic?

6. Jim Henderson. The senior TV sports anchor of our city, Jim Henderson is an articulate sports intellectual whose dignified, always brilliant sports editorials consistently are "on the money." An eloquent, precise reporter, he could have moved on to larger markets and more lucrative contracts many times over the years, but he loves this old city so much that he just can't leave. Never have I known him to be unfairly critical of anyone or anything, which is remarkable considering that our New Orleans Saints prior to 2006 had exactly one playoff victory in 39 extremely frustrating seasons, not to mention the many losing seasons of our local colleges.

7. Dr. Norman C. Francis: The president of Xavier University of Louisiana in my opinion is the most accomplished individual in our great city, if such a distinction can be singled out about any one New Orleanian. Just drive slowly along Washington Avenue and look toward the Xavier campus. The handsome old administration building was completed in 1933, I believe, when Dr. Francis was an infant and I was nine or ten. Almost every other building on that impressive (I like the green roofs) campus is a direct result of the prodigious efforts of this man.

In my younger days I didn't mind grabbing late planes after visits to NFL headquarters in New York or visiting other NFL cities as part of our effort to get an NFL franchise for our great city, or later, missions associated with the Superdome or the USFL. It might have been just a coincidence, but it seemed to me that I almost always saw a bone-weary Norman Francis on those "red-eye" flights, returning home from hustling endowments for our spectacular Xavier University of New Orleans. More than an Icon, he is a hero of New Orleans.

8. The Landrieu Family — Moon, Verna, Mary, Mark, Melanie, Michelle, Mitch, Madeleine, Martin, Melinda, and Maurice. As my friend, Stanley McDermott, says, "Moon and Verna and several of their nine children have spent a lifetime in politics, and not even the breath of a scandal anywhere." That typifies the Landrieu family. Moon is considered by many to have been our

city's greatest mayor, which is a huge compliment considering the eminent individuals such as Chep Morrison, who had such confidence in me nearly fifty years ago, and Dutch Morial, the young lawyer I hired to strike down some old Louisiana laws that needed striking down so many, many years ago, who have held that post. The Landrieu's oldest daughter, Mary, a United States senator, survived a withering, relentless attack from a well-heeled, free-spending opponent without ever losing her dignity, composure, or class. It is obvious that her superb genes have stood this impressive young woman in good stead. Her brother Mitch Landrieu, Louisiana lieutenant governor, is headed for something much bigger some day. Governor Landrieu? If so, I predict he will rank alongside John McKeithen as Louisiana's greatest governor.

9. Lindy Claiborne Boggs. Widow of the great Congressman Hale Boggs, House Majority Leader at the time of his fatal plane crash in Alaska, Lindy admirably succeeded her husband in Congress, then served later as ambassador to the Vatican. Her late husband was one of the few Southern congressmen with the political courage to vote for the Voting Rights Act of 1965, granting specific rights to our African-American citizens that they should have possessed for centuries. Lindy is the mother of the brilliant, nationally syndicated columnist Cokie Roberts, and Tommy Boggs, head of a Washington law firm.

10. John Ochsner, M.D. Here's a man who unquestionably saved my life with triple bypass open-heart surgery back in the pioneering days of the 1970s. John tells me I'm #3 on his Survivor Bypass Seniority List, and he has done thousands. He is an enormously attractive, internationally famous surgeon who has brought great fame to our city and in particular to Ochsner Foundation Hospital and to Ochsner Clinic, our city's prestigious, world-renowned medical institution founded by his famous father, Dr. Alton Ochsner. I hold no one in higher esteem, nor should our city and our state. His only weakness in life is his putting stroke.

11. Peter Finney. Peter Finney is one of America's great sportswriters and would have been a "star" in the intensely competitive New York market. Always a voice of sanity, decency, and clarity in our local sports world, he was the great sports

columnist of the old *New Orleans States* and has been the *Times-Picayune*'s featured sports columnist for many years, totaling 60 years at the newspaper.

12. Ron Forman. Everything this talented New Orleanian touches turns to gold: the Audubon Zoo, the Audubon Aquarium of the Americas, the entire Audubon Park complex, the superbly renovated golf course, his newly created Audubon Tea Room (a Mecca for everything Uptown), all great successes.

13. Doug Thornton. I have always been greatly impressed with this young man, the superb chief executive of Superdome Management Group, the highly competent management firm that operates the Louisiana Superdome for our Stadium Commission. Doug Thornton is a bright, very able young executive, extremely conscientious, a genuine Katrina hero, whose activities and sense of duty during that dreadful period already are legendary. The people who know him best hold him in awe.

14. Pete Fountain. This wonderful, gracious New Orleanian is a nationally famous musician, but I know Pete as someone who loves his city and who shows his love by a complete willingness to help a fine cause whenever called upon. Always a positive force, Pete is famous also for his Half-Fast Walking Club that trudges on foot the full route of the Rex parade on Mardi Gras Day. Pete Fountain is a New Orleanian to his toenails. He looks like one, talks like one, and he plays "When the Saints Go Marching In" better than anyone!

15. Leo Christakis. Who in the world is Leo Christakis? Leo is the proprietor of Mena's Palace, a little restaurant in the French Quarter located at the corner of Chartres and Iberville, somewhat similar in appearance to the hundreds of little neighborhood restaurants that dot our city. The food is not Galatoire's nor Antoine's, nor Commander's. It's American mixed with Creole and a touch of Greek, nothing fancy but always very, very good. Leo Christakis—like his counterparts Bozo Vodanovich, the proprietor of Bozo's in Metairie, and Leah Chase of Dooky Chase's—epitomizes New Orleans' hundreds of small restaurant owners who as a magnificent group are New Orleans icons. They serve collectively what might be the best-tasting food anywhere in the world.

16. Jimmy Fitzmorris. With great pleasure I list my dear friend Jimmy Fitzmorris, who should have been mayor and who also came very close to being governor, perhaps "out counted," many believe, for the Democratic party's nomination when that was virtually tantamount to election in Louisiana. I'll repeat Jimmy's reply when I apologized for participating in Vic Schiro's famous fireside chat that led to our great Louisiana Superdome . . . but an event that almost certainly cost Jimmy the mayor's race in 1964, his lifelong dream. Jimmy said, "David, we were good friends before that evening, and we'll always be good friends." Class.

17. Anne Milling. No list of New Orleans icons would be complete without this brilliant, beautiful "doer." Such a great civic-minded person in every respect, she has accomplished so much it would take weeks to research all her works. Her latest effort, The Women of the Storm, was comprised of top civic leaders who visited Congress after Katrina urging legislators to come see for themselves the colossal damage to our great old city. A brilliant, highly effective move!

18. Tom Benson. Like him or dislike him, love him or hate him, I cannot in good conscience leave Tom Benson off my list of New Orleans icons. He is easily our number one "icon," the most cussed and discussed person in our city's history. He "tells it like it is," sometimes a bit rudely or bluntly or incorrectly, but I know that he saved the Saints that I worked so hard so many years ago to bring to our wonderful old city. No question about it, Tom Benson represents the era that is the New Orleans Saints. On that definition alone Tom Benson is a big-time New Orleans icon.

So there you have them, my choices of New Orleans icons, absolutely in no order of rank, though I could go on forever listing the icons of this great old city.

Tough Luck with Political Leaders

Though New Orleans has been incredibly fortunate to have had such individuals contribute so richly to the city, the state as a whole has had some sad, incredible happenings and coincidences that have kept its citizens from achieving much better lives. Let's look at what has happened to Louisiana's top political leaders (we have had some very good ones) at various times during my adult life.

1. John McKeithen. No one can question that a McKeithen White House would have meant many billions of dollars to Louisiana. It also would have spared the world from the consequences of a Richard Nixon presidency.

2. Hale Boggs. Hale Boggs disappeared years ago, in 1972, in a tragic plane crash in Alaska while campaigning for a Democratic incumbent candidate. Hale was in line to be Speaker of the House at the time of his tragic loss. Without that plane crash Hale Boggs almost certainly would have become Speaker.

Boggs was a great man, one of the few Southerners in the House of Representatives who had the courage to vote for the 1965 Voting Rights Act. Plus, witnesses say that he made the "speech of his life" on the House floor endorsing this long overdue, momentous act of Congress. Also he was one of the few people in Congress with the courage to criticize J. Edgar Hoover, head of the FBI, openly. Hoover, it has been said, hated Boggs with a passion. Rumors persist in Louisiana even today that Hale Boggs' plane crash was no accident. Did *Life* ever investigate such a possibility?

3. Bob Livingston. When Bill Clinton's sexual adventures nearly cost him his presidency, Bob Livingston, Republican, was about to become Speaker of the House, an incredible rise to power for this extremely capable, likable New Orleanian and Tulane alum. An enormously able guy, he seemed to have an almost unlimited political future. He was a great favorite, incidentally, of Archbishop Philip Hannan, which would have been all the recommendation I would have needed to vote for Bob Livingston for president. Unfortunately, a couple of tactical political mistakes cost him the Speaker's post. Within a few days Bob Livingston stepped down and became a very effective lobbyist.

I've always liked Bob Livingston but his decision to step down from a likely position as Speaker of the House cost our state and city billions of dollars. He would be ranked higher than third on any list of Tough Luck Louisianians but for the loss of a possible McKeithen presidency and the loss of a man of such unquestioned stature and ability as Hale Boggs.

4. F. Edward Hébert, chairman, House Armed Services Committee. With great seniority bestowed upon him by his New Orleans constituency, plus great ability, the popular Eddie Hébert finally rose to the position of chairman of the Armed Services Committee of the House of Representatives. Almost simultaneously it became evident that an unusually large contingent of newly elected House members, Democrats and Republicans alike, were seeking reforms to the traditional seniority system of Congress.

At this point Hébert had already put into the works two billion dollars' worth of transfers of various services, activities, and bases to Louisiana, primarily New Orleans, when he decided to speak to these newcomers. According to reports he stepped to the microphone and with great confidence addressed these newly elected "rebels," many of whom had worked for years to be elected to Congress, as "Boys and Girls." His salutation was not well received. Speaking "down" to any group is instant death. It was for Eddie, who had badly misjudged his own power.

After that address, longtime efforts by the advocacy group Common Cause, which has much influence within the Democratic Party, to strip Hébert of his chairmanship eventually succeeded. Eddie Hébert resigned and came home to New Orleans, a sad and embarrassed public official. A personal tragedy for Mr. Hébert, this was an even greater blow to the economy of our area. One little slip in politics can be fatal (ask Trent Lott of Mississippi). Insiders agree that Common Cause alone could not have done him in, nor could his "Boys and Girls" statement, but the combination was deadly.

5. J. Bennett Johnston. Mary and I invited Sen. J. Bennett Johnston and his charming wife to New Orleans as our house guests over Carnival one year, probably about 1969, introducing them to many friends and acquaintances because I sensed that Bennett some day would produce great things for our state.

We were a bit surprised when Bennett voted against our

Superdome and our city on a key vote in the state senate — John McKeithen won that vote, nevertheless — but we understood that the Superdome, because of rising costs, had become unpopular in Shreveport, Johnston's hometown. He had simply voted the mood of his constituency, so no quarrel there, but I must admit that Mary and I felt that a simple telephone call explaining his position might have been in order. Later, various Superdome officials and a few lawmakers felt that Bennett Johnston built an early reputation by attacking aspects of the Superdome project, including filing a lawsuit (after I had returned to private life) aimed at the Dome's financial structure. His suit was well received in north Louisiana and perhaps in the Baton Rouge area, to Bennett's political advantage.

The lawsuit, which he lost, cost the state dearly in Superdome delays ("at least six months," according to a respected state official), but it gave Bennett statewide recognition and a voter base sufficient for him to make a strong bid for governor, losing a tight race to Edwin Edwards in late 1971. Bennett would have been a truly fine governor, as his friend and then fellow state senator, now the highly respected judge, Adrian Duplantier, has always said.

This provided the basis for a run against incumbent U.S. senator Allen Ellender, who suffered a heart attack and died during the campaign. In fairness, I believe that Bennett was going to win the race against an aging Senator Ellender anyway. After four terms, twenty-four years, as a U.S. senator, Bennett Johnston retired from the Senate to form his own lobbyist firm with his son, Hunter. He has been very successful, even if his departure should be tough luck for Louisiana in that its citizens should lose the great seniority and influence invested in Bennett Johnston.

6. Russell Long. No one can blame Russell Long for leaving the Senate at a time when his health was failing. He retired and came home to Louisiana, not to act as a lobbyist or in a lucrative "advisory" role. A tremendous figure in the Senate as chairman of the Senate Finance Committee when the Democrats were in power, he is included in this list simply because it was health and Republican administrations that caused this fine, capable

public servant to retire somewhat prematurely. A very bright, able guy, a good man. Smart as hell, actually!

7. and 8. John Breaux and Billy Tauzin. Both congressmen in positions of seniority, John Breaux and Billy Tauzin retired from Congress due to poor health. Fortunately, both of these extremely capable public servants seem to have regained their good health. They are using their retirement to work as high-powered lobbyists.

9. Chep Morrison. Chep Morrison died in a tragic plane crash in Mexico in 1964, not long after his close loss to John McKeithen in the governor's race of that year. We shall never know whether the former New Orleans mayor would have re-entered politics. If so, the entire deck of political cards would have been reshuffled. Chep Morrison was an honest, capable, top-quality Louisiana political leader who might have done great things for our state, as he certainly did for our city. His too-early loss was a sad day for Louisiana and New Orleans.

10. Edwin Edwards. What a sad waste of enormous talent. Enough said, even though I like the guy, a lot.

Has any state ever lost within a lifetime the full fruits of so many important leaders? Incredibly tough luck! Louisiana's "luck" in Washington needs to improve. All had great ability and a huge opportunity to help our state. Let's hope that our present crop of political Louisianians produces what these ten political persons came so close to producing.

Index